Jane Austen's
Emma

Jane Austen's *Emma* (1815) is at once a comedy of misunderstanding, a razor-sharp analysis of the English class system, and a classic tale of romance and moral growth that has appealed to readers and critics alike.

Taking the form of a sourcebook, this guide to Austen's much loved novel offers:

- extensive introductory comment on the contexts and many interpretations of the text, from publication to the present
- annotated extracts from key contextual documents, reviews, critical works and the text itself
- cross-references between documents and sections of the guide, in order to suggest links between contexts and criticism
- suggestions for further reading.

Part of the Routledge Guides to Literature series, this volume is essential reading for all those beginning detailed study of Emma and seeking not only a guide to the novel, but a way through the wealth of contextual and critical material that surrounds Austen's text.

Paula Byrne has a PhD from the University of Liverpool and is the author of a highly acclaimed study of *Jane Austen and the Theatre* (2002). She is now a full-time critic and biographer and is writing a life of Austen's near contemporary, the actress, novelist and poet Mary 'Perdita' Robinson.

Routledge Guides to Literature offe~   widely
studied authors and literary texts. E ts and
criticism, highlighting the range of cri t need
to be taken into consideration in adva

Routledge Guides to Literature*

Editorial Advisory Board: Richard Bradford (University of Ulster at Coleraine), Jan Jedrzejewski (University of Ulster at Coleraine), Duncan Wu (St Catherine's College, University of Oxford)

Routledge Guides to Literature offer clear introductions to the most widely studied authors and literary texts.

Each book engages with texts, contexts and criticism, highlighting the range of critical views and contextual factors that need to be taken into consideration in advanced studies of literary works. The series encourages informed but independent readings of texts by ranging as widely as possible across the contextual and critical issues relevant to the works examined and highlighting areas of debate as well as those of critical consensus. Alongside general guides to texts and authors, the series includes 'sourcebooks', which allow access to reprinted contextual and critical materials as well as annotated extracts of primary text.

Available in this series

* Some books in this series were originally published in the Routledge Literary Sourcebooks series, edited by Duncan Wu, or the Complete Critical Guide to English Literature series, edited by Richard Bradford and Jan Jedrzejewski.

Jane Austen's
Emma
A Sourcebook

Edited by Paula Byrne

Routledge
Taylor & Francis Group

LONDON AND NEW YORK

First published 2004
by Routledge
11 New Fetter Lane, London EC4P 4EE

Simultaneously published in the USA and Canada
by Routledge
29 West 35th Street, New York, NY 10001

Routledge is an imprint of the Taylor & Francis Group

Selection and editorial matter © 2004 Paula Byrne

Typeset in Sabon and Gill Sans by RefineCatch Limited, Bungay, Suffolk
Printed and bound in Great Britain by
TJ International Ltd, Padstow, Cornwall

British Library Cataloguing in Publication Data
A catalogue record for this book is available from the British Library

Library of Congress Cataloging in Publication Data
Emma – A sourcebook /
edited by Paula Byrne.
    p. cm. – (Routledge Guides to Literature)
Includes bibliographical references and index.
  1. Austen, Jane, 1775–1817. Emma – Sources. I. Byrne, Paula. II. Series.
    PR4034 . E53R68 2004
    823′.7–dc22

                                                    2003022840

ISBN 0–415–28650–6 (hbk)
ISBN 0–415–28651–4 (pbk)

Contents

Modern Criticism   48

The Work in Performance 93

3: Key Passages

Introduction 99

4: Further Reading

Annotation and Footnotes

Annotation is a key feature of this series. Both the original notes from reprinted texts and new annotations by the editor appear at the bottom of the relevant page. The reprinted notes are prefaced by the author's name in square brackets, e.g. '[Robinson's note]'.

Acknowledgements

With thanks to Duncan Wu for commissioning the book, Fiona Cairns for seeing it to press, David Leyland for word-processing assistance, Barbara Hinchcliffe for reference checking and Sandra Jones for scrupulous copy editing.

Introduction

> I could not sit seriously down to write a serious romance under any other motive than to save my life, and if it were indispensable for me to keep it up and never relax into laughing at myself or other people, I am sure I should be hung before I had finished the first chapter.[1]

Jane Austen's humorous comment about the sort of novel that she emphatically did *not* want to write belies the seriousness with which she viewed her novels and their public reception. She described *Pride and Prejudice* (1813) as 'my own darling child' and considered its heroine Elizabeth Bennet 'as delightful a creature as ever appeared in print'. *Mansfield Park* (1814) she feared would be found 'not half so entertaining' as *Pride and Prejudice*. And she worried that her latest novel *Emma* might fall between two stools: 'I am strongly haunted with the idea that to those who have preferred *Pride and Prejudice* it will appear inferior in wit, and to those who have preferred *Mansfield Park* inferior in good sense' (*Letters*, p. 306).

Emma appeared on 29 December 1815, although the title page is dated 1816. It was published by John Murray, who was at the height of his fame as Lord Byron's publisher. A memorandum in Austen's own hand has survived, recording that the novel was begun in January 1814 and completed on 29 March 1815. In that same year, she heard that the Prince Regent (later George IV) was an admirer of her work and 'kept a set of them in every one of his residences'.[2]

James Stanier Clarke, the Prince's librarian, suggested that she dedicate her next book to His Royal Highness. Jane Austen had little respect for the Prince; in particular she abhorred the shoddy way in which he had treated the Princess of Wales: 'Poor woman, I shall support her as long as I can, because she *is* a woman, and because I hate her husband' (*Letters*, p. 208). Nevertheless, she accepted the compliment to her work and (rather reluctantly) dedicated the novel to the Prince.

---

1   *Jane Austen's Letters*, ed. Deirdre le Faye (3rd edn, Oxford: Oxford University Press, 1995), p. 312. Cited hereafter as *Letters*.
2   See R. W. Chapman, *Jane Austen: Facts and Problems* (Oxford: Clarendon Press, 1948), p. 138. Cited hereafter as *Facts and Problems*.

Austen's fears for her latest 'child' were to be unfounded. Though she never earned a great deal for her novels, *Emma* was published by John Murray on a profit-sharing basis. The initial press run was 2000 and the three volumes sold for twenty-one shillings. A note in Austen's hand records a figure of £39 as 'first profits of Emma'. By October 1816, 1250 copies had been sold.[3] Perhaps more importantly, *Emma* established Austen's literary reputation. Murray, who had founded the influential *Quarterly Review*, asked Sir Walter Scott, the most celebrated novelist of the age, to review *Emma*. As we shall see, the latter's insights and observations have dogged Austen criticism and her legacy for two centuries.

Jane Austen remains one of the most popular and enduring English writers of all time, perhaps second only to Shakespeare. Like him, she has been perpetually remade into whatever suits the age in which she is read. She has been portrayed as a writer who is snobbish and elitist, but also as a dazzling satirist of snobbery and elitism. She has been represented as a hard-nosed capitalist, but also as an apologist for the women who suffered from the capitalist marriage market of her age. To some she is a political conservative, to others a feminist. She has been conceived as a patriotic nationalist and an ecological 'green'. She has even become a species of gay icon. That she can be viewed in these many guises is testament to her greatness, but this can also present problems for students trying to navigate their way in a sea of complex and seemingly contradictory criticism. The aim of this sourcebook is to demonstrate how many different critical approaches can illuminate *Emma*, but also to suggest that the best readings of the novel are those that respond to the many layers of the novel itself rather than restrict themselves to the straitjacket of theoretical 'isms'.

---

3   In the editions printed during and immediately after her death, *Pride and Prejudice* sold the very best of all, 4000 copies, compared with *Mansfield Park*, 3000, *Sense and Sensibility* and *Emma*, 2000 each, and the posthumously published joint set of *Northanger Abbey* and *Persuasion*, 2500. See *Facts and Problems*, pp. 156–7.

1

Contexts

Contextual Overview

I think I may boast myself to be, with all possible vanity, the most unlearned and uninformed female who ever dared to be an authoress.

(Jane Austen)

Writing for everybody, for nobody, for our age, for her own.

(Virginia Woolf)

Jane Austen was born on 16 December 1775 in the Hampshire village of Steventon. She was the seventh child in a family of eight, one of two daughters. The other, Cassandra, was Jane's closest friend and life-long companion. Her parents were related to the gentry class, especially on her mother's side, but they were not wealthy. Her father, the Reverend George Austen, was a clergyman of modest means, who took in schoolboys to supplement his income. The Austen children would be expected to earn their own living or marry well. The exceptions were the two brothers who lived away from home: George, who was mentally handicapped, and Edward, who was adopted by rich relatives and became a landowner and gentleman.

Jane Austen grew up in a bookish family. Her father was an avid reader with an extensive library and her mother enjoyed composing comic verses. Novels and plays were shared and read aloud together within the family circle. Jane was especially fond of novels, including those of Samuel Richardson and Henry Fielding but above all the female voices of Fanny Burney and Maria Edgeworth (see Contemporary Documents, **pp. 25–6**). Towards the end of the eighteenth century, circulating libraries and subscription libraries – the forerunners of the modern public library system – made serious reading more accessible than ever before. Novels were becoming increasingly popular, though criticized in some circles as an inferior form. In particular, romantic novels were said to have a harmful effect on the minds of young women.

Conduct books were generally considered to be the more appropriate reading material for young women. Usually written by men, often clergymen, these were etiquette manuals or sermons, which preached morals and manners. They gave advice on how women should behave during courtship and marriage, and how they should be dutiful daughters, wives and mothers. They advocated an almost impossible standard of decorum and Jane Austen had little patience with them. She particularly disliked Hannah More's novel *Coelebs in Search of a Wife* (1809), which was a thinly disguised conduct book depicting a young man who searches for a perfect wife and rejects many women on account of their moral flaws. More's perfect heroine was the kind that Austen heartily condemned: 'pictures of perfection make me sick and wicked' (*Letters*, p. 335). She much preferred the flawed heroines of Fanny Burney and Maria Edgeworth. In *Pride and Prejudice* the unattractively prim Mary Bennet quotes trite moral epithets from conduct books at wholly inappropriate moments. The habit does not endear her to her family or the reader. Likewise, the odious clergyman Mr Collins is shocked that the Bennet sisters would rather read novels than volumes such as the sermons of Dr Fordyce (the flavour of which is represented by an extract here – see Contemporary Documents, **pp. 23–4**).

Austen herself was an ardent champion of the novel. In Chapter 5 of *Northanger Abbey* (1818), she defended her fellow novelists as 'an injured body'. 'No species of composition', she continued, 'has been so much decried'. Burney and Edgeworth are then cited as exemplars of great novelists: 'it is only *Cecilia, Camilla*, or *Belinda*; or, in short, only some work in which the most thorough knowledge of human nature, the happiest delineation of its varieties, the liveliest effusions of wit and humour are conveyed to the world in the best chosen language'.[1]

When she joined a subscription library in 1798, she wrote that hers was a family of 'great novel readers and not ashamed of being so' (*Letters*, p. 26). The name of 'Miss J. Austen, Steventon' duly appears in the list of subscribers published in Fanny Burney's novel *Camilla* (1796). Her reading habits were not confined to novels: her favourite poet was William Cowper and she profoundly admired the prose of Dr Johnson. She was also influenced by her brothers' immersion in the dramatic tradition – Shakespeare of course, but also contemporary playwrights such as Richard Brinsley Sheridan and a popular and skilful, though now neglected, female playwright called Hannah Cowley.

James and Henry Austen, the brothers to whom Jane was closest, loved writing and acting. They staged plays in the Steventon barn with the schoolboys that lived at the parsonage and other neighbouring families. When the Austens' exotic French cousin, Eliza de Feuillide, came to stay at the parsonage she joined in the theatrical party. Together they performed some of the best comedies of the eighteenth century, including *The Rivals* (1775), *Tom Thumb* (1730) and *The Wonder: A Woman Keeps a Secret* (1725). One of the great misconceptions about Jane Austen is that she disliked and distrusted theatre and the dramatic arts. This is principally due to the débâcle over private theatricals in *Mansfield Park* where an adaptation of a notoriously licentious play, *Lovers' Vows*, is performed. In fact, Austen was fascinated by the theatre, was a keen and discerning theatre-goer all

---

1   See *Northanger Abbey* in *The Novels of Jane Austen*, ed. R. W. Chapman, 5 vols (3rd edn, Oxford: Oxford University Press, 1932–34), vol. 5, p. 38.

her life, and was deeply influenced by the dramatic tradition in her writing. One intriguing possible source for *Emma* is Dibdin's *The Birth-Day* (1799), based on Kotzebue's play *Reconciliation*; it has a heroine called Emma Bertram who lives with an invalid father and finally marries a family friend (see Contemporary Documents, **p. 26**).

James and Henry Austen particularly relished comedies that satirized the cult of 'feeling' that was sweeping the nation. This was the age of sensibility, where the capacity for delicacy of feeling and acute emotion, whether of joy or sorrow, was regarded as a mark of true refinement and even moral rectitude. Sensibility signalled not only aesthetic responsiveness to both art and nature, but also instinctive human sympathy towards one's fellow beings. The particular manifestations of sensibility were considered to be those bodily responses that were linked to the emotions, such as blushing, tears and swooning. Mental illness – the kind of breakdown that Marianne Dashwood seems to suffer in *Sense and Sensibility* – was sometimes seen as a symptom of excessive sensibility. The seminal European novels of sensibility were Goethe's *Sorrows of Young Werther* (1774), Rousseau's *La Nouvelle Héloïse* (1761), and Oliver Goldsmith's *The Vicar of Wakefield* (1766). The latter (see **p. 22**), in which the tender-hearted vicar is reduced to tears at frequent intervals, is the book that Harriet Smith lends to Robert Martin in *Emma*.

The eighteenth century was at the same time the age of 'reason' or 'enlightenment'. Advances in both empirical science and moral philosophy made it an era in which humankind's capacity for rational thought was celebrated. So it was that in Austen's lifetime a contention between rationalism and feeling was clearly apparent. Plays such as Sheridan's *The Rivals* depicted the harmful effects of excessive sensibility, a theme which Jane Austen was also to explore in her first published novel, *Sense and Sensibility* (1811). James and Henry Austen founded their own literary magazine, *The Loiterer*, which made it a point of principle to burlesque 'novel slang' and the absurdities of popular sentimental fiction. Many of their stories satirize characters who feign sensibility in order to achieve their own ends, but come hilariously unstuck.

Jane Austen soaked up this atmosphere and, encouraged by her family, began her own career in writing at an early age. It is always fascinating to read the apprentice work of a great writer. Virginia Woolf was perhaps the first to see in Austen's early work or 'juvenilia' the seeds of her genius: 'The girl of fifteen is laughing, in her corner, at the world'. Austen was especially keen to amuse her sophisticated, theatre-loving, burlesque-writing brothers. Many of her short early works are dedicated to them. She was brought up in a household full of lively boys and her juvenilia reveals her as a high-spirited young girl unafraid to make jokes about death, debauchery and violence. Her heroines are thieves, liars and drunkards, who are not above poisoning, maiming and even murdering their rivals. Many of these early pieces are extremely funny, combining slapstick with verbal incongruities. In one story, three families grow so close they do not 'scruple to kick one another out of the window on the slightest provocation'. In another, two sisters debate the future happiness of another sister: 'Yet how can I hope that my sister may accept a man who cannot make her happy?' – 'He cannot, it is true, but his fortune, his name, his house, his carriage will.' Jane Austen's keen sense of the absurd stayed with her throughout her writing career.

Perhaps the best of the juvenilia is a short satire of sensibility entitled 'Love and Freindship' [*sic*] (see Contemporary Documents, **pp. 19–21**). As in *The Loiterer*, the satirical target is indulgence or luxuriance in excessive emotion for its own sake. Austen's two heroines blush, swoon and burst into tears on a whim to show the physical evidence of their sensibility, but in reality they are selfish and hypocritical. Possessing few moral scruples, they scheme and connive and ride roughshod over their victims whilst pretending to be virtuous and sweet. When the heroines are caught red-handed stealing from their host, they pretend that their personal integrity has been violated by the intrusion. They lie, cheat and steal all in the name of sensibility. On witnessing the deaths of their lovers in a road accident, they follow the rules of sensibility: 'Two gentlemen most elegantly attired but weltering in their own blood was what first struck our eyes . . . Sophie shrieked and fainted on the ground – I screamed and instantly ran mad.' The world that Austen presents in her juvenilia is sometimes anarchic and disturbing, but almost always uproariously funny.

One of the assumptions that has been made about Jane Austen is that she was immovably attached to village life, and consciously chose in her novels not to engage with the political and historical events of her time. This view of 'gentle' Jane was initiated by her brother Henry's posthumous biographical notice, in which he described his sister's life as uneventful: 'A life of usefulness, literature, and religion, was not by any means a life of event'. Similarly, his insistence that she 'never uttered a hasty, a silly, or a severe expression' is belied by the caustic wit of her letters and juvenilia in which quite a different Jane emerges. It is understandable that a bereaved brother would remember only the very best qualities of his beloved sister, but it is erroneous to depict her as a writer who does not engage with her historical and political context.

Jane Austen lived through one of the most eventful periods in modern history, a time of revolution and war. In her lifetime, England lost the American War of Independence, the French Revolution was sparked by the storming of the Bastille, and the Revolutionary and Napoleonic Wars were fought for over twenty years (1792–1815). The horror of the French Revolution was brought directly to Austen's door when the husband of her beloved cousin, Eliza de Feuillide, was guillotined in 1794, when Jane was 19. Eliza later married Jane's brother, the Reverend Henry Austen. Jane's naval brothers Francis and Charles were often in peril during the Revolutionary and Napoleonic Wars. *Emma* was finished in the same year that the conflict came to a climax with the battle of Waterloo.

This was, furthermore, the era of the industrial and agrarian revolutions. Mr Knightley practises the new agricultural system of crop rotation. Critics have often quoted Austen's remark that 'three or four families in a country village is the very thing to work on' (though it should be remembered she was referring here to someone else's work – she was giving advice to her niece, a novice writer), but she was acutely aware that hers was a society in flux, culturally, politically and socially. Social mobility is one of her major themes.

Critics have now acknowledged that political and historical issues subtly infiltrate the polite drawing rooms of Jane Austen's novels. In *Persuasion* (1818), the war reports are discussed and the novel ends with the heroine (now a sailor's wife) in 'dread of a future war'. In *Emma*, Austen examines ideas of Englishness and patriotism by means of the contrasts between the manners of George Knightley and Frank Churchill. Whereas Knightley (his name itself the same as St George, the patron saint of England) epitomizes 'the true English style' of few words and 'nothing of ceremony', Frank Churchill is associated with French gallantry, verbal wit and charm, especially by Knightley whose jealousy manifests itself in his 'Frankophobia'.

In *Emma* the controversial issue of the abolition of the slave trade also hovers in the air. After a twenty-year campaign, a bill outlawing the slave trade finally reached parliament in 1807. Jane Austen herself was in favour of the abolition, as was her brother Francis. When Jane Fairfax compares the oppression of African slaves with the slavery of women, Mrs Elton, a native of the slave port of Bristol, is quick to respond: 'Oh my dear, human flesh! You quite shock me; if you mean a fling at the slave trade, I assure you Mr Suckling was always rather a friend to the abolition' (see **p. 129**). In 1792, Mary Wollstonecraft had famously made the connection between slaves and women in her *Vindication of the Rights of Woman* (see Contemporary Documents, **pp. 24–5**). As Jane Austen was well aware, single women on the marriage market with little economic security or prospects were exceedingly vulnerable. In a letter she half-joked 'single women have a dreadful propensity for being poor – one thing in favour of marriage'. But when her own opportunity for material comfort and financial security came in an offer of marriage to a suitable and wealthy young man whom she did not love, she ultimately turned him down. Though she earned some financial independence from her novels, in the main she was dependent on her father and then her brothers for economic security. Jane Austen's world was far from being a haven of domestic security: it was rife with insecurities and fears.

In 1801, her parents announced that they were retiring to Bath, taking their daughters with them. Jane was devastated to be leaving the family home and many of her possessions – her books and her piano had to be sold. For the next five years, there is a silence surrounding her. Few letters from this period survive, and she apparently put her writing on hold. In 1804–5, she began work on a new novel about a family called 'The Watsons', then abandoned it after her father died in 1805. This has been seen in an early version of *Emma*, since the heroine, also called Emma, is motherless with an invalid father (see Contemporary Documents, **pp. 21–2**). This novel fragment is much bleaker than any of her other works, and depicts the humiliating and painful plight of aging and impoverished spinsters searching for husbands. Emma's younger sisters argue over the single men in the neighbourhood, while her eldest sister has been left bitter and depressed from a failed romance. Emma herself has been cut off from her aunt's inheritance and is a 'weight upon [her] family, without a sixpence'.

It was only when Jane (along with her mother and sister) moved to Chawton in Hampshire after her father's death that she began revising her work in earnest. *Sense and Sensibility* was published in 1811, *Pride and Prejudice* in 1813, *Mansfield Park* in 1814, and *Emma* in 1815.

Austen took a keen interest in what other people thought of her work, compiling a list of criticism and praise (see Contemporary Documents, **pp. 17–19**). She did not, however, take seriously the advice given to her by the Prince Regent's librarian, Mr Clarke, when he recommended ideas for her new novel, including a portrayal of a clergyman based on himself. In response to his suggestion that she should undertake a 'Historical Romance', she wrote back kindly but firmly that she could not 'write a serious Romance . . . No – I must keep to my own style and go on in my own way'. Nevertheless, Clarke's letter inspired her to write a three-page satire of a romance novel entitled 'Plan of a Novel, According to Hints from Various Quarters', in which she mockingly follows his advice and that of her friends.[2] She proposes a ludicrous plot, which ends up with the heroine fleeing with her father to Russia. The heroine is of course perfect: 'a faultless character herself – perfectly good, with much tenderness and sentiment, and not the least wit'. This was not the kind of novel she was interested in at all, and this parody gives us an insight into her own artistic intentions. Emma Woodhouse is the very reverse of a faultless character.

Placing Jane Austen in her literary and cultural context is not easy. Confusingly, she is often studied alongside the 'Romantic' writers. Whilst her own creative period did coincide with that of William Wordsworth, Samuel Taylor Coleridge, Lord Byron and Walter Scott, she was in many ways an anti-Romantic writer. Romanticism is itself a slippery term to define, but there were many respects in which it grew from 'sensibility', a literary and cultural movement of which we have already seen Austen being critical. As she said herself, she could not write a romance to save her life, and her novels constantly set out to deflate literary traditions such as the Gothic novel, the novel of sensibility, the romance. Her final unfinished novel 'Sanditon' shows her continuing interest in literary parody. Sir Edward Denham is a pseudo-Byronic figure, ludicrously quoting the Romantic poetry of Scott, Burns and Wordsworth, and living out fantasies from the novels he reads.

At the end of 'Plan of a Novel' Austen writes emphatically, 'the name of the work *not* to be called *Emma*'. Here she alludes to the fact that her latest novel is not to be considered in the same genre as 'romance'. It satirizes the conventions of the Romantic novel: Emma Woodhouse marries not a mysterious, handsome stranger but a familiar, plain-speaking fraternal figure. Far from escaping to Russia and encountering wicked villains on the way, Emma rarely leaves Highbury and has never seen the sea. One has only to compare *Emma* with Walter Scott's novel of the same year, *The Antiquary*, to see the differences in content and style. *The Antiquary* fulfils the criteria of the 'Historical Romance', though it skilfully combines the Gothic, supernatural elements with wonderful comic characters. A glance at a short descriptive passage also reveals the rich, evocative language that the poet-turned-novelist incorporated into the Romantic novel:

---

2   See *Minor Works*, ed. R. W. Chapman, revised by B. C. Southam (London: Oxford University Press, 1975), pp. 428–30.

The sun was now resting his huge disk upon the edge of the level ocean, and gilded the accumulation of towering clouds, through which he had travelled the livelong day, and which now assembled on all sides like misfortunes and disasters around a sinking empire and falling monarch. Still, however, his dying splendour gave a sombre magnificence to the massive congregation of vapours, forming out of their unsubstantial gloom the show of pyramids and towers, some touched with gold, some with purple, some with a hue of deep and dark red.

(Scott, *The Antiquary*, vol. 1, ch. 7)

The language here is very similar to that of a famous description of a mountainous cloudscape in Wordsworth's *The Excursion*, published just over a year before. Setting, style and tone are all a very long way from the contained world of Austen's Highbury. Yet despite their differences of style and content, Austen greatly admired Scott and joked that it was unfair that he wrote such good novels: 'he has fame and profit enough as a Poet, and should not be taking the bread out of other people's mouths. – I do not like him, and do not mean to like *Waverley*.'

As Scott was able to recognize in his own analysis of Austen's work, they were very different kinds of writer: he writes deprecatingly of his own 'Big Bow-wow strain' in contrast to her realism and subtlety (see Interpretations, **p. 40**). Of course, his praise for her realism has left an uneasy legacy in that Austen is often praised for what she didn't do as much as for what she did. Nevertheless, what Scott and others following him realized was that Jane Austen's innovations within the form of the novel were truly pioneering. Her art paved the way for the great realist novelists of the Victorian age, such as George Eliot and Henry James.

Chronology

Bullet points are used to denote events in Jane Austen's life, and asterisks to denote historical and literary events.

1775
* (16 December) Jane Austen born at Steventon in Hampshire, seventh child of the Reverend George Austen (1731–1805) and Cassandra Leigh (1739–1827)
* American War begins with Battles of Lexington, Concord and Bunker Hill

1776
* Adam Smith's *The Wealth of Nations* published (intellectual foundation of capitalist economics)
* Declaration of American Independence
* James Watt begins work on steam engine

1778
* France declares war on the side of the American rebels
* Death of Jean-Jacques Rousseau, whose praise of nature and protest against society, expressed in his *Social Contract* (1761) and *Discourse on Inequality* (1754), proved influential in provoking a revolutionary state of mind; Fanny Burney's *Evelina* published

1783
* At age 7, JA sent to boarding school in Oxford (then moved to Southampton), with her sister Cassandra; falls gravely ill with fever and is brought home
* Treaty of Paris acknowledges American Independence
* Pitt the Younger becomes Prime Minister

1784
* Private theatricals in Hampshire; Sheridan's *The Rivals* 'performed by some young ladies and Gentlemen at Steventon'
* Dr Johnson dies

1785

- Jane and Cassandra sent to the Abbey school in Reading; return home in 1786
* Invention of power loom by Edmund Cartwright

1786–7

- Austen family visited by JA's cousin, Eliza de Feuillide (god-daughter and possibly natural daughter of Warren Hastings, Governor of Bengal)

1787–9

- Private theatricals revived, with Eliza de Feuillide. JA begins writing her juvenilia
* Byron born (1788)

1789

* Fall of the Bastille, 14 July, and the beginning of the French Revolution which, under the ideals of 'liberté, égalité, fraternité', eventually saw the end of the French monarchy and the aristocratic domination of French society, but at the expense of the reign of Terror (1793–94)
* Blake publishes *Songs of Innocence*

1790

- JA writes 'Love and Freindship' [*sic*], dedicated to Eliza
* Edmund Burke's *Reflections on the Revolution in France* published

1791

- Edward Austen (later Knight) marries. The youngest Austen child, Charles, leaves home at age 12 to join Portsmouth Naval Academy
* Boswell's *Life of Johnson* published; Thomas Paine, political theorist who signposted the path of the American colonies' independence, publishes *The Rights of Man, Part 1*
* Anti-revolutionary 'Church and King' riots in Birmingham – radical philosopher and scientist Joseph Priestley has his house ransacked

1792

- Eliza visits Steventon, reporting news of the 'tragical events' in France
* Mary Wollstonecraft (mother of Mary Godwin, later Mary Shelley) writes *A Vindication of the Rights of Woman*

1793

* Board of Agriculture established for the improvement of the depressed rural economy
* Publication of William Godwin's radical treatise on *Political Justice*

1794

- Eliza de Feuillide's husband arrested and guillotined in Paris; she manages to flee to safety

*   Blake, *Songs of Experience*; Ann Radcliffe's Gothic novel, *The Mysteries of Udolpho* published

1795

•   'Elinor and Marianne' written (first version of *Sense and Sensibility*). JA meets and begins flirtation with Tom Lefroy. Starts working on *First Impressions* (first version of *Pride and Prejudice*)

*   Keats born

*   Prince of Wales marries Caroline of Brunswick

1797

•   JA begins revising 'Elinor and Marianne' as *Sense and Sensibility*. Tom Fowle, Cassandra's fiancé, dies; Henry Austen marries Eliza de Feuillide

•   *First Impressions* ('about the length of Miss Burney's Evelina') offered to London publisher Thomas Cadell by George Austen, but declined

*   Mary Wollstonecraft dies giving birth to Mary Shelley; Burke dies; Commons reject abolition of slavery

1798

•   *Susan* (first version of *Northanger Abbey*) probably begun

*   Publication of Wordsworth and Coleridge's *Lyrical Ballads*

1799

•   JA's aunt Mrs Leigh Perrot is accused of stealing a card of expensive lace in a haberdashery, awaits trial for grand larceny and is confined to the gaolkeeper's squalid lodge for seven months; Mrs Austen offers to send her daughters to keep her company, but is refused, due to appalling conditions; Mrs Leigh Perrot is found innocent

•   Frank and Charles on active naval service in the Mediterranean. Frank promoted to post-captain in 1800

1800

*   Act of Union with Ireland

1801

•   Austens move to Bath

*   Fall of Pitt; temporary peace with France

1802

•   Jane Austen accepts, then rejects, marriage proposal from Harris Bigg-Wither, a family friend

*   Truce between Britain and France, but war is renewed a year later

1803

•   *Susan* (later *Northanger Abbey*) sold to the publisher Crosby for £10

1804

- On JA's birthday, one of her closest friends. Madam Lefroy, is killed in a road accident
* Napoleon crowned Emperor of France

1805

- Reverend George Austen dies after a brief illness
- 'Lady Susan' (short epistolary novel, not published by Austen) written; also abandons novel-fragment 'The Watsons', begun in the previous year
* The naval Battle of Trafalgar thwarts French invasion plans; Nelson's death in action makes the figure of the sailor into the ultimate national hero

1806

- Austens leave Bath for Clifton with 'happy feelings of escape'; they spend next months travelling, before settling at Castle Square, Southampton

1807
* Slave trade abolished

1809

- Austens move to Chawton, Hampshire, to a cottage on a substantial estate inherited by Edward from the Knights
- JA buys back the manuscript of *Susan* from Crosby

1811

- *Mansfield Park* begun (February); *Sense and Sensibility* published (November)
* George III declared insane; Regency begins under George, Prince of Wales
* 'Luddite' attacks in countryside – disaffected agricultural labourers break machines

1812
* Byron 'awakes to find himself famous' upon publication by John Murray of the first two cantos of *Childe Harold's Pilgrimage*

1813

- *Pride and Prejudice* published by Egerton (January)
- November: second editions of *Pride and Prejudice* and *Sense and Sensibility*, following good sales
* Byron's Oriental verse romance *The Giaour* published; also Coleridge's Gothic drama *Remorse* and Percy Shelley's politically radical long poem, *Queen Mab*

1814

- Jane Austen begins writing *Emma* in January; *Mansfield Park* is published by Egerton in May

* Walter Scott, after highly successful career writing verse romances, anonymously publishes his first novel, *Waverley*
* Publication of William Wordsworth's long poem *The Excursion*, regarded in its own time as his major achievement
* Napoleon abdicates

1815
* *Emma* completed in March and published by John Murray in December
* Napoleon escapes from Elba, is defeated by Wellington at the Battle of Waterloo

1816
* JA working on *Persuasion*; ill for much of the year

1817
* JA begins her unfinished last novel, 'Sanditon'; in May is moved to Winchester for medical treatment
* JA dies on 18 July in Winchester and is buried in the cathedral

1818
* *Northanger Abbey* and *Persuasion* published by Murray, with Memoir of JA by her brother
* also published: final part of Byron's *Childe Harold*, William Hazlitt's *Lectures on the English Poets*, Scott's *Rob Roy*, Mary Shelley's *Frankenstein*
* Cassandra destroys most of her sister's large correspondence

Contemporary Documents

From **Opinions of *Emma*: Collected and Transcribed by Jane Austen** (1816), reprinted in the *Works of Jane Austen*, ed. R. W. Chapman, 6 vols (Oxford: Oxford University Press, 1923–54), vol. VI, *Minor Works*, pp. 436–9; also in *Jane Austen: The Critical Heritage*,[1] ed. B. C. Southam, 2 vols (London: Routledge & Kegan Paul, 1968–87), vol. I, pp. 55–7

Jane Austen was interested in what her family and friends thought of her latest novel and copied out their comments, probably in 1816. 'P & P' and 'M P' refer to her previous two novels, *Pride and Prejudice* and *Mansfield Park*. The responses provide a fascinating insight into the preoccupations of Austen's original readers: an interest in character is paramount, but there are also responses to language and to the novel's truth to nature (what we would now call its 'realism' is the reason why Captain Austen likes it, but also the reason why Mrs Guiton does not – she presumably had a taste for more exotic 'romance'). Many later readers and critics have had similar responses to the characters: admiration for the soundness of Mr Knightley, delight in the comic portrayals of Miss Bates and Mrs Elton, a certain feeling that we do not get to know Jane Fairfax well enough. Comments such as that of Austen's relatives Mr and Mrs Leigh Perrot, 'thought Frank Churchill better treated than he deserved', suggest that the novel provoked moral debate in its immediate circle of reader just as it has in the critical tradition and the academic classroom.

Captain Austen. – liked it extremely, observing that though there might be more Wit in P & P – & an higher Morality in M P – yet altogether, on account of it's [*sic*] peculiar air of Nature throughout, he preferred it to either.

Mrs F. A. – liked & admired it very much indeed, but must still prefer P & P.

Mrs J. Bridges – preferred it to all the others.

Miss Sharp – better than M P – but not so well as P & P – pleased with the Heroine

---

1   Hereafter cited as *CH*.

for her Originality, delighted with Mr K – & called Mrs Elton beyond praise. – dissatisfied with Jane Fairfax.

Cassandra – better than P & P – but not so well as M P.

Fanny K. – not so well as either P & P or M P – could not bear *Emma* herself. – Mr Knightley delightful. – Should like J. F. – if she knew more of her.

Mr & Mrs J. A. – did not like it so well as either of the 3 others. Language different from the others; not so easily read.

Edward – preferred it to M P. – *only*. – Mr K. liked by every body.

Miss Bigg – not equal to either P & P – or M P – objected to the sameness of the subject (Match-making) all through. – Too much of Mr Elton & H. Smith. Language superior to the others.

My Mother – thought it more entertaining than M P – but not so interesting as P & P – No characters in it equal to Ly Catherine & Mr Collins.

Miss Lloyd – thought it as *clever* as either of the others, but did not receive so much pleasure from it as from P & P – & M P.

Mrs & Miss Craven – liked it very much, but not so much as the others.

Fanny Cage – like it very much indeed & classed it between P & P – & M P.

Mr Sherer – did not think it equal to either M P – (which he liked the best of all) or P & P. – Displeased with my pictures of Clergymen.

Miss Bigg – on reading it a second time, liked Miss Bates much better than at first, & expressed herself as liking all the people of Highbury in general, except Harriet Smith – but could not help still thinking *her* too silly in her Loves.

The family at Upton Gray – all very much amused with it. – Miss Bates a great favourite with Mrs Beaufoy.

Mr and Mrs Leigh Perrot – saw many beauties in it, but could not think it equal to P & P – Darcy & Elizabeth had spoilt them for anything else. – Mr K. however, an excellent Character; Emma better luck than a Matchmaker often has. – Pitied Jane Fairfax – thought Frank Churchill better treated than he deserved.

Countess Craven – admired it very much, but did not think it equal to P & P. – which she ranked as the very first of it's [sic] sort.

Mrs Guiton – thought it too natural to be interesting.

Mrs Digweed – did not like it so well as the others, in fact if she had not known the Author, could hardly have got through it.

Miss Terry – admired it very much, particularly Mrs Elton.

Henry Sanford – very much pleased with it – delighted with Miss Bates, but thought Mrs Elton the best-drawn Character in the Book. – Mansfield Park however, still his favourite.

Mr Haden – *quite* delighted with it. Admired the Character of Emma.

Miss Isabella Herries – did not like it – objected to my exposing the sex in the character of the Heroine – convinced that I had meant Mrs & Miss Bates for some acquaintance of theirs – People whom I never heard of before.

Miss Harriet Moore – admired it very much, but M P still her favourite of all.

Countess Morley – delighted with it.

Mr Cockerelle – liked it so little, that Fanny would not send me his opinion.

Mrs Dickson – did not much like it – thought it *very* inferior to P & P. – Liked it the less, from there being a Mr & Mrs Dixon in it.

Mrs Brandreth – thought the 3d vol: superior to anything I had ever written – quite beautiful!

Mr B. Lefroy – thought that if there had been more Incident, it would be equal to any of the others. – The Characters quite as well drawn & supported as in any, & from being more everyday ones, the more entertaining. – Did not like the Heroine so well as any of the others. Miss Bates excellent, but rather too much of her. Mr & Mrs Elton admirable & John Knightley a sensible Man.

Mrs B. Lefroy – rank'd *Emma* as a composition with S & S. – not so *Brilliant* as P & P – nor so *equal* as M P. – Preferred Emma herself to all the heroines. – The Characters like all the others admirably well drawn & supported – perhaps rather less strongly marked than some, but only the more natural for that reason. – Mr Knightley[,] Mrs Elton & Miss Bates her favourites. – Thought one or two of the conversations too long.

Mrs Lefroy – preferred it to M P – but like [*sic*] M P. the least of all.

Mr Fowle – read only the first & last Chapters, because he had heard it was not interesting.

Mrs Lutley Sclater – liked it very much, better than M P – & thought I had 'brought it all about very cleverly in the last volume.'

Mrs C. Cage wrote thus to Fanny – 'A great many thanks for the loan of *Emma*, which I am delighted with. I like it better than any. Every character is thoroughly kept up. I must enjoy reading it again with Charles. Miss Bates is incomparable, but I was nearly killed with those precious treasures! They are Unique, & really with more fun than I can express. I am at Highbury all day, & I can't help feeling I have just got into a new set of acquaintance. No one writes such good sense. & so very comfortable.'

Mrs Wroughton – did not like it so well as P & P. – Thought the Authoress wrong, in such times as these, to draw such Clergymen as Mr Collins & Mr Elton.

Sir J. Langham – thought it much inferior to the others.

Mr Jeffery (of the Edinburgh Review) was kept up by it three nights.

Miss Murden – certainly inferior to all the others.

Capt. C. Austen wrote – 'Emma arrived in time to a moment. I am delighted with her, more so I think than even with my favourite Pride & Prejudice, & have read it three times in the Passage.'

Mrs D. Dundas – thought it very clever, but did not like it so well as either of the others.

From **Jane Austen, 'Love and Freindship'** [*sic*] (1790), reprinted in *The Works of Jane Austen*, ed. R. W. Chapman, 6 vols (Oxford: Oxford University Press, 1923–54), vol. VI, *Minor Works*, revised by Brian Southam, 1975, pp. 93–4

In 1790, when Jane Austen was 15, she wrote a short comic novel called 'Love and Freindship' [*sic*], which she dedicated to her cousin, Eliza de Feuillide. 'Love and Freindship' is a parody of the sentimental novel and shows Austen satirizing many of the literary conventions of the time. In this passage, we see how the two (anti-)heroines, Laura and Sophia, use and abuse sensibility to justify their selfish and malicious behaviour. By invoking the code of sensibility, they are able to persuade a naïve young girl to abandon the man she really loves in order to elope with an unprincipled fortune hunter. Although the scene is comic, and the characters' behaviour delightfully absurd, we also witness their destructive interference in a young girl's happiness, which is twisted into the appearance of a noble and generous act. Here, we can see glimpses of Austen's interests as a mature writer: one of Emma's most potentially serious misdemeanours is her attempt to separate Harriet Smith from Robert Martin. The story is written in the form of letters, almost all of them (including the one from which this extract is taken) penned by the witty but mischievous Laura.

[. . .] To Macdonald-Hall, therefore, we went, and were received with great kindness by Janetta the daughter of Macdonald, & the Mistress of the Mansion. Janetta was then only fifteen; naturally well disposed, endowed with a susceptible Heart, and a simpathetic Disposition, she might, had these amiable Qualities been properly encouraged, have been an ornament to human Nature; but unfortunately her Father possessed not a soul sufficiently exalted to admire so promising a Disposition, and had endeavoured by every means in his power to prevent its encreasing with her Years. He had actually so far extinguished the natural noble Sensibility of her Heart, as to prevail on her to accept an offer from a young man of his Recommendation. They were to be married in a few months, and Graham, was in the House when we arrived. *We* soon saw through his Character. – He was just such a Man as one might have expected to be the choice of Macdonald. They said he was Sensible, well-informed, and Agreable; we did not pretend to Judge of such trifles, but as we were convinced he had no soul, that he had never read the Sorrows of Werter,[1] & that his Hair bore not the slightest resemblance to Auburn, we were certain that Janetta could feel no affection for him, or at least that she ought to feel none. The very circumstance of his being her father's choice too, was so much in his disfavour, that had he been deserving her, in every other respect yet *that* of itself ought to have been a sufficient reason in the Eyes of Janetta for rejecting him. These considerations we were determined to represent to her in their proper light & doubted not of meeting with the desired success from one naturally so well disposed, whose errors in the Affair had only arisen from a want of proper confidence in her own opinion, & a suitable contempt of her father's. We found her indeed all that our warmest wishes could have

---

1   A reading of Goethe's epistolary novel of unrequited love, *The Sorrows of Young Werther* (1774), was an absolute prerequisite for the development of a character of true 'sensibility'. On being denied his beloved Charlotte – who is married to another – Werther takes his own life. Such was the power of the novel that, so rumour had it, suicide became a fashionable pursuit for young men all over Europe. There is, alas, little evidence for the truth of the rumour: but the novel's influence on subsequent literature was enormous.

hoped for; we had no difficulty to convince her that it was impossible she could love Graham, or that it was her duty to disobey her Father.

From **Jane Austen, 'The Watsons'** (1804), reprinted in *The Works of Jane Austen*, ed. R. W. Chapman, 6 vols (Oxford: Oxford University Press, 1923–54), vol. VI, *Minor Works*, pp. 324–5, 328–9, 342, 361–2

This work has been seen as an early version of *Emma*. The heroines share the same Christian name, their mothers are dead and they have an invalid father. The one important difference is that Emma Watson is poor and insecure about her status in society. 'The Watsons' is much darker than *Emma*, which is perhaps one of the reasons why Austen abandoned it. Nevertheless, the plight of unmarried women in society is a theme that she returns to again and again.

This matter was settled, & they went to Dinner. – 'Your Father, Miss Emma, is one of my oldest friends – said Mr Edwardes, as he helped her to wine, when they were drawn round the fire to enjoy their Desert, – We must drink to his better health. – It is a great concern to me I assure you that he should be such an Invalid. – I know nobody who likes a game of cards in a social way, better than he does; & very few people that play a fairer rubber. – It is a thousand pities that he should be so deprived of the pleasure. For now we have a quiet little Whist club that meets three times a week at the White Hart, & if he c^d but have his health, how much he w^d enjoy it.' 'I dare say he would Sir – & I wish with all my heart he were equal to it.' 'Your Club w^d be better fitted for an Invalid, said Mrs E. if you did not keep it up so late.' – This was an old greivance. – [. . .]
  Emma in the meanwhile was not unobserved, or unadmired herself. – A new face & a very pretty one, could not be slighted – her name was whispered from one party to another, & no sooner had the signal been given, by the Orchestra's striking up a favourite air, which seemed to call the young Men to their duty, & people the centre of the room, than she found herself engaged to dance with a Brother officer, introduced by Capt. Hunter. – Emma Watson was not more than of the middle height – well made & plump, with an air of healthy vigour. – Her skin was very brown, but clear, smooth and glowing –; which with a lively Eye, a sweet smile, & an open Countenance, gave beauty to attract, & expression to make that beauty improve on acquaintance. – Having no reason to be dissatisfied with her partner, the Even^g began very pleasantly to her; & her feelings perfectly coincided with the reiterated observation of others, that it was an excellent Ball.
  [. . .] – Emma concluded her narration. – 'And so, you really did not dance with Tom M. at all? – But you must have liked him, you must have been struck with him altogether.' – 'I do *not* like him, Eliz: –. I allow his person & air to be good – & that his manners to a certain point – his address rather – is pleasing. – But I see nothing else to admire in him. – On the contrary, he seems very vain, very

conceited, absurdly anxious for Distinction, & absolutely contemptible in some of the measures he takes for becoming so. – There is a ridiculousness about him that entertains me – but his company gives me no other agreable Emotion.' 'My dearest Emma! – You are like nobody else in the World.' [. . .]

The change in her home society, & stile of life in consequence of the death of one friend and the imprudence of another had indeed been striking. From being the first object of hope & solicitude of an uncle who had formed her mind with the care of a parent, & of tenderness to an aunt whose amiable temper had delighted to give her every indulgence, from being the life & spirit of a house, where all had been comfort & elegance, and the expected heiress of an easy independence, she was become of importance to no one, a burden on those, whose affection she could not expect, an addition in an house, already over-stocked, surrounded by inferior minds with little chance of domestic comfort, & as little hope of future support.

From **Oliver Goldsmith, *The Vicar of Wakefield*** (1766), ed. Arthur Friedman (Oxford: Oxford University Press, 1991), pp. 158–9

> The book that Harriet Smith gives Robert Martin to read in *Emma* was one of the most popular sentimental novels of the eighteenth century. Goldsmith later regretted his choice of sentimental plot, which consciously aimed to produce tears of sympathy for the suffering of the virtuous. The novel charts the follies and misfortunes of the unworldly Vicar of Wakefield and his family. Towards the end, the vicar has been imprisoned for debt, his daughter has reportedly died from a broken heart as a result of a disastrous marriage, his other daughter Sophia has been abducted by a villain, and his son is threatened with the gallows.

'In all our miseries,' cried I, 'what thanks have we not to return, that one at least of our family is exempted from what we suffer. Heaven be his guard, and keep my boy thus happy to be the supporter of his widowed mother, and the father of these two babes, which is all the patrimony I can now bequeath him. May he keep their innocence from the temptations of want, and be their conductor in the paths of honour'. I had scarce said these words, when a noise, like that of a tumult, seemed to proceed from the prison below; it died away soon after, and a clanking of fetters was heard along the passage that led to my apartment. The keeper of the prison entered, holding a man all bloody, wounded and fettered with the heaviest irons. I looked with compassion on the wretch as he approached me, but with horror when I found it was my own son. – 'My George! My George! And do I behold thee thus. Wounded! Fettered! Is this thy happiness! Is this the manner you return to me! O that this sight could break my heart at once and let me die!'

From **John Gregory, *A Father's Legacy to his Daughters*** (London, 1774), p. 30

Writers such as John Gregory and James Fordyce recommended attractive modes of behaviour that should be practised and cultivated by women during courtship and marriage. Here, in his celebrated *A Father's Legacy to his Daughters*, Gregory warns against the dangers of wit, and describes the tribulations of spinsterhood. Austen depicts the 'unprotected situation of an old maid' in the character of Miss Bates, but she is far removed from the peevish, bitter creature of Gregory's description.

Conduct and Behaviour

Wit is the most dangerous talent you can possess. It must be guarded with great discretion and good nature, otherwise it will create you many enemies. Wit is perfectly consistent with softness and delicacy; yet they are seldom found united. Wit is so flattering to vanity, that they who possess it become intoxicated, and lose all self-command.

Friendship, Love, Marriage

I am of opinion that you may attain a superior degree of happiness in a married state, to what you can possibly find in any other. I know the forlorn and unprotected situation of an old maid, the chagrin and peevishness which are apt to infect their tempers, and the great difficulty of making a transition with dignity and chearfulness [*sic*], from the period of youth, beauty, admiration, and respect, into the calm, silent, unnoticed retreat of declining years. [. . .] In short, I am of opinion, that a married state, if entered into from proper motives of esteem and affection, will be the happiest for yourselves, make you most respectable in the eyes of the world, and the most useful members of society.

From **James Fordyce, *The Character and Conduct of the Female Sex and the Advantages to be Derived by Young Men from the Society of Virtuous Women*** (London, 1776), pp. 82–3

Ah, my female friends, did you in particular, did you but know, how deeply the male heart is enchanted with those women, whose conversation presents the picture of simplicity and grace, of ease and politeness, in a group, the spirit of whose conversation is a compound of sprightliness, sense and modesty; who seldom dispute, and never wrangle; who listen with attention to the opinions of others, and deliver their own with diffidence, more desirous of receiving than of giving conviction, more ambitious to please than to conquer! Such, believe me, are sure of conquering in the noblest sense.

From **Mary Wollstonecraft, *A Vindication of the Rights of Woman*** (1792), reprinted in Mary Wollstonecraft, *Political Writings,* ed. Janet Todd (Oxford: Oxford University Press, 1994), pp. 235–6

Mary Wollstonecraft (1759–97) was a radical writer and polemicist on behalf of the 'rights' of women. She challenged the conduct book view of women as naturally weak and yielding creatures, concerned with frivolous and superficial accomplishments, and advocated the importance of education and equality. In this passage she recommends that children should show a sense of duty towards their parents, without becoming dominated to an unhealthy degree. She makes the point that women, more than men, are taught from an early age to be slaves to their parents and thus readily submit themselves to the slavery of marriage.

Duty to Parents

The simple definition of the reciprocal duty, which naturally subsists between parent and child, may be given in a few words: The parent who pays proper attention to helpless infancy has a right to require the same attention when the feebleness of age comes upon him. But to subjugate a rational being to the mere will of another, after he is of age to answer to society for his own conduct, is a most cruel and undue stretch of power; and, perhaps, as injurious to morality as those religious systems which do not allow right and wrong to have any existence, but in the Divine will. [. . .]

Females, it is true, in all countries, are too much under the dominion of their parents; and few parents think of addressing their children in the following manner, though it is in this reasonable way that Heaven seems to command the whole human race. It is your interest to obey me till you can judge for yourself; and the Almighty Father of all has implanted an affection in me to serve as a guard to you whilst your reason is unfolding; but when your mind arrives at maturity, you must only obey me, or rather respect my opinions, so far as they coincide with the light that is breaking in on your own mind.

A slavish bondage to parents cramps every faculty of the mind; and Mr Locke very judiciously observes, that 'if the mind be curbed and humbled too much in children; if their spirits be abased and broken much by too strict an hand over them; they lose all their vigour and industry.'[1] This strict hand may in some degree

---

1   Quoting John Locke, *Some Thoughts Concerning Education* (1693).

account for the weakness of women; for girls, from various causes, are more kept down by their parents, in every sense of the word, than boys. The duty expected from them is, like all the duties arbitrarily imposed on women, more from a sense of propriety, more out of respect for decorum, than reason; and thus taught slavishly to submit to their parents, they are prepared for the slavery of marriage.[2]

From **Fanny Burney, Camilla; or A Picture of Youth** (1796); reprinted ed. Edward A. Bloom and Lilian D. Bloom (Oxford: Oxford University Press, 1983), pp. 84 and 110–11

> Austen was a great admirer of Burney's work, and in *Northanger Abbey* cites both *Cecilia* (1782) and *Camilla* (1796) as exemplars of 'genius, wit and taste'. Camilla Stanley, like Emma Woodhouse, is a flawed heroine, whose main defect is 'an imagination that submitted to no control'. Burney's hero, Edgar, is captivated at the sight of Camilla holding a baby in her arms. In *Emma*, a serious quarrel between Emma and Mr Knightley is smoothed over when he sees his baby niece being dandled in Emma's arms.

The beauty of Camilla, though neither perfect nor regular, had an influence so peculiar on the beholder, it was hard to catch its fault; and the cynic connoisseur, who might persevere in seeking it, would involuntarily surrender the strict rules of his art to the predominance of its loveliness. Even judgment itself, the coolest and last betrayed of our faculties, she took by surprize, though it was not till she was absent the seizure was detected. Her disposition was ardent in sincerity, her mind untainted with evil. The reigning and radical defect of her character – an imagination that submitted to no control – proved not any antidote against her attractions; it caught, by its force and fire, the quick-kindling admiration of the lively; it possessed, by magnetic pervasion, the witchery to create sympathy in the most serious. [. . .]

Camilla at length, wholly out of breath, gave over; but perceiving that the baby was no longer at its mother's breast, flew to the poor woman, and, taking the child in her arms, said: 'Come, I can nurse and rest at the same time; I assure you the baby will be safe with me, for I nurse all the children in our neighbourhood.' She then fondled the poor little half-starved child to her bosom, quieting, and kissing, and cooing over it.

Miss Margland was still more incensed; but Edgar could attend to her no longer. Charmed with the youthful nurse, and seeing in her unaffected attitudes, a thousand graces he had never before remarked, and reading in her fondness for children the genuine sweetness of her character, he could not bear to have the pleasing reflections revolving in his mind interrupted by the spleen of

---

2 For further reading see Adriana Craciun (ed.), *A Routledge Literary Sourcebook on Mary Wollstonecraft's* A Vindication of the Rights of Woman (London: Routledge, 2002).

Miss Margland, and slipping away, posted himself behind the baby's father, where he could look on undisturbed, certain it was a vicinity to which Miss Margland would not follow him.

From **Thomas Dibdin, *The Birth-Day*, translated and adapted from August von Kotzebue** (1799), in *A Collection of Farces and Other Afterpieces Selected by Mrs Inchbald,* 7 vols (London, 1809), vol. II, p. 8

Austen has sometimes been perceived as hostile to theatre, yet, as her letters reveal, she enjoyed going to the professional theatres of London and Bath.[1] In 1799, she saw Dibdin's *The Birth-Day*, which was based on Kotzebue's play *Reconciliation*. The plot is centred on a family feud, which is eventually resolved by cousins, who fall in love. The heroine, Emma Bertram, is devoted to her father and, as with Emma Woodhouse, is persuaded to marry with the caveat that the married couple live in her father's house.

Emma: Don't you think my father will live to be a very old man now?
Harry: If he is careful not to exert himself too much.
Emma: That shall be my care.
Harry: And will you always remain with him?
Emma: Always, always.
Harry: But if other duties should call upon you?
Emma: Other duties! What duties can be more sacred?
Harry: The duties of a wife or mother.
Emma: No – I never intend to marry.
Harry: Never marry?
Emma: Not if I should be obliged to leave my father.
Harry: Your husband would supply the place of a son.
Emma: And the son would take the daughter from the father.
Harry: But if a man could be found who would bestow on your father a quiet old age, free from every sorrow; who, far from robbing the father of a good daughter, would weave the garland of love round three hearts, who would live under his roof and multiply your joys, by reconciling your father and your uncle.

1   See Paula Byrne, *Jane Austen and the Theatre* (London: Hambledon and New York: Palgrave, 2002).

From **Hannah More, *Strictures on the Modern System of Female Education*,** 2 vols (London, 1799), vol. I, pp. 142–3, vol. II, pp. 103–4

Though Jane Austen had little patience for over-moralizing conduct literature, she was well aware of the widespread popularity of writers such as Hannah More. As noted earlier, More's novel *Coelebs in Search of a Wife*, enormously popular for a brief period, depicts the kind of perfect heroine that Austen heartily condemned. Here, in *Strictures*, More censures female wit and advocates 'a submissive temper and a forbearing temper'. More warns young women against the dangers of female friendship, especially if the wrong sort of friend is chosen: if Emma Woodhouse had got around to reading the appropriate litera-ture, she might have chosen Jane Fairfax as her companion rather than Harriet Smith.

An early habitual restraint is peculiarly important to the future character and happiness of women. They should when very young be inured to contradiction. Instead of hearing their bon-mots treasured up and repeated to the guests till they begin to think it dull, when they themselves are not the little heroine of the theme, they should be accustomed to receive but little praise for their vivacity or their wit, though they should receive just commendation for their patience, their indus-try, their humility, and other qualities which have more worth than splendour. They should be led to distrust their own judgment; they should learn not to murmur at expostulation; but should be accustomed to expect and to endure opposition. It is a lesson with which the world will not fail to furnish them; and they will not practise it the worse for having learnt it the sooner. It is of the last importance to their happiness in life that they should early acquire a submissive temper and a forbearing spirit. They must even endure to be thought wrong sometimes, when they cannot but feel they are right. [. . .]

The propensity of mind which we are considering, if unchecked, lays its posses-sors open to unjust prepossessions, and exposes them to all the danger of unsounded attachments. In early youth, not only love, but friendship, at first sight, grows out of an ill-directed sensibility; and in afterlife, women under the powerful influence of this temper, conscious that they have much to be borne with, are too readily inclined to select for their confidential connections, flexible and flattering companions, who will indulge and perhaps admire their faults, rather than firm and honest friends, who will reprove and would assist in curing them. We may adopt it as a general maxim, that an obliging, weak, yielding, complaisant friend, full of small attentions, with little religion, little judgment, and much natural acquiescence and civility, is a most dangerous, though generally a too much desired confidante: she soothes the indolence, and gratifies the vanity of her friend, by reconciling her to her own faults, while she neither keeps the understanding nor the virtues of that friend in exercise.

2

Interpretations

Introduction

Like Shakespeare, with whom she has been compared, the elusive and myriad-minded Jane Austen is re-made by each age. The 'Gentle Jane' of the late Victorian era was replaced in the twentieth century with other more intellectually rigorous though often contradictory manifestations. In the 1950s, she was seen as an anti-social 'good hater', whose caustic wit thinly masked the bitterness of her world view. In the 1970s, she was arch-defender of the kinds of conservative and trad-itionalist values embodied in the Tory country estate. At the extreme ends of political interpretation, she has been seen as an upholder of both capitalist and Marxist ideologies. In the 1980s she was a champion of female politics, a sub-versive writer engaging with the feminist ideology of her time.

Emma in particular has lent itself to multiple critical readings. Austen's depic-tion of a strong female protagonist with status, money and power has stimulated gender-based and feminist criticism. The novel's interest in letters, word-games and riddles has lent itself to deconstructive and post-modern readings. Its contrast between French and English manners has provoked debate about nationalism and patriotism.

I have limited the critical extracts to those that deal specifically with *Emma*. Some important works on Austen which do not refer in detail to *Emma* are, however, mentioned in the introduction and given a full reference. For example, two influential books by Mary Lascelles (1939) and Mary Poovey (1984), which transformed critical thinking on Austen, have not been included because neither refers to *Emma* in detail, nor do they lend themselves to representation in brief extracted form.

Jane Austen did herself no favours when she described her writing style to her nephew Edward as 'the little bit (two-inches wide) of ivory on which I work with so fine a brush, as produces little effect after much labour' (*Letters*, p. 323)[1]. Her modest and self-deprecating comment has been partially responsible

---

1   *Jane Austen's Letters*, ed. Deirdre le Faye (3rd edn, Oxford: Oxford University Press, 1995). Cited hereafter as *Letters*.

for the way in which she has been perceived as a writer who is limited in scope. However, the very first critics of her work defined her narrative style in a similar way. When other contemporary writers attempted to define Austen's essence, so different from their own, they resorted to the metaphor of drawing upon a small canvas; she was said to resemble the 'Flemish' school of painting or to have a 'Chinese delicacy'. The word 'miniaturist' comes up again and again.

This image of Jane Austen was in no small measure initiated and has been greatly sustained by the critical reception of *Emma*. The most public of her novels, it was dedicated to the Prince Regent by demand, and was the first of her novels to receive a major review from a leading author of the day: the writer and poet Sir Walter Scott (1771–1832). In contrast to her other novels, *Emma* is set in one place, the small village of Highbury. The heroine has never seen the sea. There are no visits to London, Portsmouth, Bath or Lyme Regis.

As a writer who was constantly experimenting with different types of heroines and different types of setting, Austen would later exchange the small country village of *Emma* for the Royal spa town of Bath in *Persuasion*. In her final, unfinished novel 'Sanditon' she chose a bustling, trendy seaside resort. Yet Austen has gained the reputation for being a novelist of small things. The oft-quoted remark that she made to her would-be-writer niece, Anna, again seems to confirm this view: 'three or four families in a country village is the very thing to work on' (*Letters*, p. 275). Yet again, Austen's own words seem to limit her, though, as with her words to Edward, it is important to remember that she was reflecting more on her correspondent's writing than her own. A far less frequently quoted piece of advice in the same letter to Anna reads 'your descriptions are often more minute than will be liked – you give too many particulars of right hand and left.' Yet *Emma* has long played a large part in the perception of Austen as a writer of limited scope, and Scott's review left a legacy that was only challenged by the enormous transformations in literary criticism of the late twentieth century.

Austen's very first critics emphasized her 'realism', that is her ability to 'copy' or convey the impression of 'real life'. The politically conservative *British Critic* praised *Emma*'s realism as a refreshing change from 'fanatical books' by 'fanatical authoresses'.

Scott's review of *Emma* saw that in presenting 'ordinary life', Austen was writing a very different kind of novel from what had gone before. Other early reviewers stressed similar aspects to Scott, using words such as 'ordinary', 'middling classes', 'homeliness', and 'domestic', pointing out that Austen writes not about the castle but the 'country house'. It is striking that Austen has acquired the reputation of an elitist writer concerned with the upper classes, yet one of her pioneering achievements, from the perspective of her first critics and readers, was her representation of 'ordinary people'.

The Romantic poet Coleridge admired Austen, but his fellow-poet Wordsworth was less impressed: 'though he admitted that her novels were an admirable copy of life, he could not be interested in productions of that kind; unless the truth of nature were presented to him, clarified, as it were, by the pervading light of the imagination, it had scarce any attractions in his eyes'.[2] For Charlotte Brontë (1816–55), too, Austen lacked passion. Picking up on Scott's comments, she declares: 'there is a Chinese fidelity, a miniature delicacy in the painting: she ruffles her reader by nothing vehement, disturbs him by nothing profound: the Passions are perfectly unknown to her' (see **p. 43**). Brontë's comments were made in response to the political liberal writer George Henry Lewes (1817–78), who was a great admirer of Austen. Lewes once argued that 'the truthful representation of character' was 'the highest department of the novelist's art'. As he picks up on the analogy of miniaturist painting, Lewes again makes an important appraisal of Jane Austen in 1859: 'Such art as hers can never grow old, never be superseded. But, after all, miniatures are not frescoes, and her works are miniatures'.

Despite Scott's and Lewes's acknowledgement of Austen as a major writer, she received little critical attention until the 1870 *Memoir of Jane Austen* written by her nephew, Edward. This created a cult of 'gentle Jane', provoking the famous outburst from Henry James, 'their "dear," our dear, everybody's dear, Jane' (see **p. 48**). In the late 1860s, Julie Kavanagh and Margaret Oliphant wrote reviews that praised Austen as an ironist, although their essays largely went unnoticed. For Kavanagh, 'she saw and painted with a touch so fine that we often do not perceive its severity'.[3] Oliphant distinguished 'a fine vein of feminine cynicism' and 'a fine stinging yet soft-voiced contempt'.[4] But it was Richard Simpson's essay in the *North British Review* (1870) that was the first to argue that Austen's irony was at the very foundation of her genius (see **p. 46**). He presented a powerful counter-image to the 'dear Aunt Jane' of the 1870 *Memoir*, arguing that she was a serious, committed writer, who was interested in her craft and whose artistic concerns were rooted in her early burlesques and satires. Austen was an 'ironical censurer' who consciously rejected the 'poetic faculty' in favour of 'humour', 'delicacy of analysis' and 'subtlety of thought or language'.

In the twentieth century, *Emma* was usually regarded as the climax of Austen's achievement. For A. C. Bradley, it was 'a comedy, unsurpassed . . . among novels'. For R. W. Chapman, it was Austen's 'masterpiece' (as well as a detective novel).[5] Reginald Farrer described it as 'the Book of Books' (see **p. 51**). Anticipating the formalism or 'New Criticism' of the mid-twentieth century, Farrer discussed the technical mastery of *Emma*. The difficulty for Austen in creating a heroine such as Emma, he suggested, was that she had to balance sympathetic identification with critical detachment; she had to be both inside and outside her main character.

The first writer to offer a substantial academic study of Austen's novels was Mary Lascelles in *Jane Austen and Her Art* (1939). Taking issue with the patronizing attitude exemplified by male critics, Lascelles gave a detailed

2 See *Jane Austen: The Critical Heritage*, ed. B. C. Southam, 2 vols (London: Routledge and Kegan Paul, 1968–87), vol. I, p. 117, cited hereafter as *CH*.
3 See Julia Kavanagh, 'Miss Austen's Six Novels', in *English Women of Letters* (1862), pp. 251–74.
4 See Mrs Oliphant, 'Miss Austen and Miss Mitford', *Blackwood's Edinburgh Magazine* (March 1870), vol. cvii, pp. 294–305.
5 See R. W. Chapman, *Jane Austen: Facts and Problems* (Oxford: Clarendon Press, 1948), pp. 201–5.

examination of Jane Austen's technical and artistic technique, and portrayed her as first and foremost a 'writer'. It is no exaggeration to say that Lascelles's analysis of Austen's art marked a new development in Austen criticism. Austen's pre-eminence in the literary canon was then secured by influential critics such as F. R. Leavis (see **p. 56**) and Ian Watt, who placed her at the forefront of the novel tradition. The 'New Criticism' reached its heights in the 1940s and 1950s. Its approach was largely ahistorical, focusing upon the literary work in its own right – although some readings were informed by other disciplines such as psychology and sociology. Thus the influential American critic Wayne Booth analysed Austen's technical brilliance (see **pp. 63–4**) and her development of 'free indirect speech', whereas the critic and psychologist D. W. Harding presented her as a subversive author whose writing was her way 'of finding some mode of existence for her critical attitudes' (see **pp. 53–4**). For Harding, her 'hatred' was so 'regulated' that most readers failed to see it, and her books were 'read and enjoyed by precisely the sort of people whom she disliked'. Harding's psychoanalytical view of Austen's suppression and displacement was not popular amongst Austen's devoted readers, but it was vitally important in shaking off the complacency of the view of her as a comfortable and uncritical writer.

Other writers also began to see her as subversive. Marvin Mudrick followed a similar line to that of Harding when he argued that irony was Austen's 'defence and discovery' (**pp. 57–9**). Emma's supposed reformation is the ultimate irony of a novel steeped in irony. Though both Mudrick and the influential New York critic Edmund Wilson (see **pp. 54–5**) found glancing intimations of lesbianism in Emma's infatuation with Harriet Smith, the image of Austen as a somewhat severe moralist was difficult to shake off. According to Dr Leavis, Austen does not offer an ' "aesthetic" value that is separable from moral significance': 'without her intense moral preoccupation she wouldn't have been a great novelist' (see **p. 56**). Lionel Trilling's liberal-minded approach to *Emma* may be seen as a more humane version of Leavis's moral vision: 'To represent the possibility of controlling the personal life, of becoming acquainted with ourselves, of creating a community of "intelligent love" – this is indeed to make an extraordinary promise and to hold out a rare hope' (see **pp. 59–61**).

The predominantly moral and formalistic approach to Austen was modified in the 1970s by two important books that located her novels in their historical, literary and political context. Alistair Duckworth's *The Improvement of the Estate* (1971) (see **pp. 65–6**) and Marilyn Butler's *Jane Austen and the War of Ideas* (1975) (see **pp. 66–7**) represented Austen as a conservative writer who was opposing innovation and change in a time of revolution. Both critics drew upon the writing of the politician Edmund Burke,[6] in particular his opposition to

---

6   Edmund Burke (1729–97) was a Whig politician and writer. Though committed to political liberty, as indicated by his support of the American Revolution, he shocked his friends and supporters by his opposition to the French Revolution. The intention of his *Reflections on the Revolution in France* (1790) was to counter the threat of French disorder to British stability. Burke used the metaphor of damage and violation to the estate and home to illustrate the horrors of the Revolution. He advocated hierarchical structures embodied in the aristocracy and the clergy, and upheld the values and traditions of the ruling classes.

the French Revolution, to show Austen engaging in the political 'war of ideas'. Though ground-breaking in many respects, Duckworth's and Butler's approach was still traditional and formalist in methodology, in so much as it appealed to authorial intention and used close-reading techniques.

Duckworth and Butler's literary-historical approach relied upon the use of binary oppositions, such as conservative versus radical, anti-Jacobin versus Jacobin.[7] Some overtly Marxist critics, by contrast, agreed with the depiction of Austen as a polemical Tory, but were more concerned with the deeper or more 'structural' ideological implications of her purported views. Thus Raymond Williams in his *The Country and The City* (1973) located Austen as a vitally important writer who was writing at a crucial time when the split between 'culture' and 'society' widened. Another Marxist, David Aers, took a harsh view of Austen's capitalist values and bourgeois ideology: he attacked Duckworth's non-evaluative stance, suggesting that it was the critic's business to be critical of Burkean ideology (which Aers, of course, viewed as rife with contradictions). For Aers, Mr Knightley is an arch capitalist and Austen's treatment of the disenfranchised – 'the poor', the gypsies and even Jane Fairfax – typifies her bourgeois complacency (see **pp. 73–5**).

A far more balanced view of Austen's class attitudes is articulated by Juliet McMaster and Julia Prewitt Brown. McMaster suggests how class is aligned to manners in *Emma*, and emphasizes Austen's corrective treatment of Emma's snobbish attitudes (see **pp. 86–7**). Mr Knightley is presented as a character who patently does not exploit his rank. For Julia Prewitt Brown, the novel is presented 'not from the perspective of frozen class division' but from that of 'living change'. The novel is full of upward and downward social mobility: 'It is not France in the 1780s, but England at the beginning of the nineteenth century' (see **pp. 68–9**). Critics influenced by the growth of 'cultural history' in the late twentieth century, such as Edward Copeland, placed Austen within a commodity culture and suggested how she used shopping to explore society (**pp. 88–9**). In *Emma*, the action moves forward by its display of consumerism, from dining tables and carriages to ribbons and gloves.

A different group of late twentieth-century critics approached Austen's novels from the perspective of post-structuralist theory. Rather than adopting an author-centred approach, post-structuralists, especially practitioners of 'deconstruction', were concerned with language and textuality. Their interest is in what language does and cannot do, rather than what meaning the author intended to convey. The author is rejected and the 'text' is unravelled to reveal gaps, contradictions and indeterminacies that are taken to 'subvert' the surface intention. Readings of this kind have made much of the word-games, charades, riddles and letters that

---

7 The 'Jacobins' were the extreme revolutionaries, particularly associated with Robespierre and Danton, who came to dominate Paris in the mid-1790s and who turned the Revolution to the Terror. 'Jacobinical' thus became a term of abuse for English sympathizers with the French Revolution (such as the young Wordsworth and Coleridge). 'Anti-Jacobin' was the name adopted by British politicians and journalists of the late 1790s who vigorously opposed those whom they regarded as unpatriotic, not to say traitorous revolutionary Francophiles.

characterize *Emma* as a linguistically self-conscious text. Joseph Litvak, for example, traces a network of puns to show the instability of language and explores the relationship between games and reading in *Emma* (see **pp. 76–7**), while Valentine Cunningham plays with the various meanings of the word 'Frank' to reveal the instability of language in the novel: 'At the core of *Emma* is "the so unfrank doings of the unfrank franker of unfrank letters" ' (**pp. 83–4**).

If this approach inherits some of the dangers of formalism, in ignoring the world beyond the text, the 'New Historicism' sought to redefine the boundaries of historical enquiry. New Historicist critics drew upon the work of Michel Foucault, who saw history in terms of power. Nancy Armstrong in her *Desire and Domestic Fiction* argued that Austen's novels were prime agents in the construction of 'bourgeois subjectivity', that is to say an emphasis on the primacy of individual liberty and self-expression – values considered to be central to, and distinctive of, not only eighteenth-century political and moral thought (the 'Enlightenment') but also western liberal society more generally (see **pp. 77–8**). The eighteenth-century domestic novel, which took over from the conduct book, showed the emergence of a new kind of domestic woman, whose value existed in personal virtue rather than status. According to this reading, in *Emma*, the emphasis on the need for literacy based on polite speech produces a new and bourgeois form of cultural authority, which readers emulated.

Perhaps the most important contribution to modern Jane Austen studies has come from feminist criticism. Feminists have rescued Austen from the image of a Tory, anti-feminist writer that Marilyn Butler presented in *The War of Ideas*. In the highly influential, jointly written study *The Madwoman in the Attic* (1979), Sandra Gilbert and Susan Gubar founded a repressed and subversive feminist hidden behind the prim surface of the Austen image. They argued that it was as if against her own better instincts that Austen ultimately conformed to patriarchy. By their account, Austen punished her lively and spirited heroine by uniting her with Knightley, thus condemning her to a life of 'silence and service' (see **pp. 70–1**). Conversely, Margaret Kirkham attempted to place Austen in the camp of radical feminists, such as Mary Wollstonecraft. More judiciously, Claudia Johnson argued in her brilliantly written and scrupulously argued study *Jane Austen: Women, Politics and the Novel* that the novels arose out of a strong tradition of subversive women writers who smuggled social criticism into their novels (see **pp. 80–1**). *Emma* allows Austen to explore positive versions of female power. Rather than endorsing patriarchy, the novel ends with a marriage between equals. Furthermore, in sharing Emma's home, Knightley gives his blessing to her rule. In her own more recent work, Johnson has moved to gender-oriented criticism, re-examining notions of sexuality by 'historicizing the treatment of femininity and masculinity in *Emma*', and linking these ideas to questions of patriotism and national identity.

Feminist and gender-oriented critics have shown how Austen, far from being just a 'miniaturist', was engaging with the political, literary and social climate of her time. The long wars with France and the background of the French Revolution informed her ideas on nationalism and patriotism. Critics have drawn attention to the contrasts between the very English George Knightley and the

Francophile Frank Churchill. Knightley's interest in agricultural improvement makes him a progressive farmer, aware of the country's war-time food supplies. But his attachment to the soil and the people is evident in his refusal to engage in acts of enclosure (see **pp. 117–18**).[8] The importance of a harmonious balance between nature and agriculture – 'English verdure, English culture, English comfort' – is emphasized by ecocritic Jonathan Bate (see **pp. 89–90**). And, returning full circle to the origins of the critical tradition, Miranda Burgess has suggested that Walter Scott's review of *Emma* implicitly identified Austen as the mother of the novel and thus himself as, in a manner of speaking, her literary son. In so doing, 'for the first time he granted literary history an explicitly national importance' (see **pp. 92–3**).

---

8   During the years 1760–1830, a series of Parliamentary laws called the 'Enclosure Acts' were passed to further reform agricultural production by consolidating small, widely spread lots of land into larger plots. Although historians vigorously debate the economic effects of enclosure, there is no doubt that the movement was perceived as infringement on the common land rights of the many for the sake of the increased prosperity of the few.

Early Critical Reception

Most of the extracts in this section are reprinted in B. C. Southam, *Jane Austen: The Critical Heritage*, 2 vols (London: Routledge & Kegan Paul, 1968–87), cited hereafter as *CH*.

From **Walter Scott, unsigned review of *Emma*,** in *Quarterly Review*, vol. 14 (dated October 1815, issued March 1816), pp. 188–201. Reprinted in *CH*, pp. 58–69

Austen's new publisher John Murray was also the founder of the *Quarterly Review* and he invited Walter Scott to 'dash off an article on *Emma*'. This review was a watershed for Austen, bringing a notable increase in her reputation as a literary writer. Scott's extensive review, which also included comments on *Pride and Prejudice* and *Sense and Sensibility*, was the first significant analysis of her work. Murray had warned Scott that *Emma* lacked 'incidence and romance', but Scott did not agree, writing that it had 'cross-purposes enough (were the novel of a more romantic cast) for cutting half the men's throats and breaking all the women's hearts'. More significantly, Scott saw that Austen was a pioneering writer who had created a novel that was essentially anti-romantic and 'realistic'. It was nothing like his own novelistic style, which he later described (see **p. 40**) as the 'big Bow-wow strain'.

Scott begins his review with a précis of the novel, and places *Emma* in its literary context. He bemoans the excesses of the sentimental and romantic novel; 'robbers, smugglers, bailiffs, caverns, dungeons and mad-houses, have been all introduced until they ceased to interest'. Scott thus describes the new style of 'realistic' novel, of which *Emma* is the exemplar: 'the art of copying from nature as she really exists in the common walks of life, and presenting to the reader, instead of the splendid scenes of an imaginary world, a correct and striking representation of that which is daily taking place around him'. Like other early critics, Scott points out that Austen was also a pioneering writer for drawing characters and incidents 'more immediately from the current of ordinary life than was permitted by the former rules of the novel'. In other words, rather than writing inspirational literature about elevated characters in exceptional circumstances, Austen wrote about ordinary people in ordinary circumstances.

In this review, Scott's famously compared Austen's art with the Flemish school of painting: 'The subjects are not often elegant, and certainly never grand; but they are finished up to nature, and with a precision which delights the reader'. Similarly, he drew a landscape analogy to explain her works: rather than sublime mountains, we have cornfields and cottages. Other critics would follow Scott in perceiving Austen as a limited writer, even though he so passionately admired 'the exquisite touch which renders ordinary commonplace things and characters interesting from the truth of the description and the sentiment'.

Accordingly, a style of novel has arisen, within the last fifteen or twenty years . . . neither alarming our credulity nor amusing our imagination by wild variety of incident . . . the substitute for these excitements . . . was the art of copying from nature as she really exists in the common walks of life, and presenting to the reader, instead of the splendid scenes of an imaginary world, a correct and striking representation of that which is daily taking place around him. [. . .]

We, therefore, bestow no mean compliment upon the author of *Emma*, when we say that, keeping close to common incidents, and to such characters as occupy the ordinary walks of life, she has produced sketches of such spirit and originality, that we never miss the excitation which depends upon a narrative of uncommon events, arising from the consideration of minds, manners, and sentiments, greatly above our own. In this class she stands almost alone; for the scenes of Miss Edgeworth[1] are laid in higher life, varied by more romantic incident, and by her remarkable power of embodying and illustrating national character. But the author of *Emma* confines herself chiefly to the middling classes of society; her most distinguished characters do not rise greatly above well-bred country gentlemen and ladies; and those which are sketched with most originality and precision, belong to a class rather below that standard. [. . .]

[. . .] The object of most young ladies is, or at least is usually supposed to be, a desirable connection in marriage. But Emma Woodhouse, either anticipating the taste of a later period of life, or, like a good sovereign, preferring the weal of her subjects of Highbury to her own private interest, sets generously about making matches for her friends without thinking of matrimony on her own account. [. . .]

[. . .] there are cross-purposes enough (were the novel of a more romantic cast) for cutting half the men's throats and breaking all the women's hearts. But at Highbury Cupid walks decorously, and with good discretion, bearing

---

1 Maria Edgeworth, author of *Belinda* and other novels admired by Austen.

his torch under a lanthorn, instead of flourishing it around to set the house on fire. [. . .]

The author's knowledge of the world, and the peculiar tact with which she presents characters that the reader cannot fail to recognize, reminds us something of the merits of the Flemish school of painting. The subjects are not often elegant, and certainly never grand; but they are finished up to nature, and with a precision which delights the reader.

[. . .] Upon the whole, the turn of this author's novels bears the same relation to that of the sentimental and romantic cast, that cornfields and cottages and meadows bear to the highly adorned grounds of a show mansion, or the rugged sublimities of a mountain landscape. It is neither so captivating as the one, nor so grand as the other, but it affords to those who frequent it a pleasure nearly allied with the experience of their own social habits; and what is of some importance, the youthful wanderer may return from his promenade to the ordinary business of life, without any chance of having his head turned by the recollection of the scene through which he has been wandering.

From **Walter Scott on Jane Austen, journal entry,** 14 March 1826

That young lady had a talent for describing the involvement and feelings and characters of ordinary life which is to me the most wonderful I ever met with. The Big Bow-wow strain I can do myself like any now going, but the exquisite touch which renders ordinary commonplace things and characters interesting from the truth of the description and the sentiment is denied to me.

From **Unsigned review of *Emma* in *The Champion*,** 31 March 1816, pp. 102–3, reprinted in *Nineteenth-Century Fiction*, vol. 26, no. 4 (March, 1972), pp. 469–74

> This review praises *Emma* for its accurate depiction of 'ordinary' life amongst the 'middling classes'. The novel is distinguished from other contemporary sentimental novels by its interest in domestic scenes without appealing to pathos. Austen's style is admired for its simplicity and modesty, as is her subject matter; she chooses the country house for her characters, rather than the great hall or castle.

The imitative arts – and novel-writing is the art of imitating in a narrative the scenes of life – are productive of two distinct gratifications; – one, arising from the intrinsic beauty of grandeur of the objects represented, and the other, from the skill of the artist, shown in representing objects of an ordinary, and at the same time so familiar a nature, as to invite an easy comparison between the prototype and the imitation, and to draw the intellectual faculties into a pleasing criticism on the merits of his imitative efforts. The latter, rather than the former, is the principal attraction which we hold out to our readers in recommending to them the volumes before us. One rare merit which they possess, is an entire freedom from anything like the pretence or technicality of authorship. – Their style is easy, unaffected, and fluent. Simple elementary affections of middling life, and the little obvious peculiarities of character, are all which the authoress (for they are the work of a lady) pretends or professes to exhibit. Those who exclusively estimate the value of a work of fiction by its appeals to the more elevated feelings, and its display of the complex machinery of dark passions and imaginative sensations, will find very little to their taste, we fear, in the homely pictures of these volumes. Even of the sober pathos of domestic affliction, there is very little for the senti- mental reader. – Lively sketches of comfortable home-scenes – graphic details of the localities of provincial life – pictures of worthy affections, unassuming amusements and occupations, and most spirited and racy touches of the gro- tesque peculiarities which diversify human character, are the claims which our authoress puts forth to popularity. She presents nature and society in very unornamented hues; and yet, so strong is the force of nature, that we will venture to say, few can take up her work without finding a rational pleasure in the recog- nitions which cannot fail to flash upon them of the modes of thinking and feeling which experience every day presents in real life. Her scenes have the advantage of being of that middling stamp, which come within the observation of a very large proportion of readers. The country house is no castle or hall of honour, – but a plain mansion, with a shrubbery and large gates, such as every one knows at the top of a populous village, looked up to as the great house of the place; and when we are occasionally transported to London, our authoress has the originality to waive Grosvenor or Berkeley-squares, and set us down in humble Brunswick- square. There is a corresponding modesty in her characters. If we take her own description of them, one is 'rational and unaffected,' another, 'straight-forward and open-hearted;' and the heroine herself, who gives title to the work, is content with being 'handsome, clever, and rich;' – to which we will add, lively, conceited, and rather proud, but benevolent, amiable, volatile, – and addicted to a very extraordinary occupation for a young lady, by no means *hors de combat* – being only twenty-one – viz. that of matchmaking. The scrapes and entanglements in which she involves herself in the pursuit of this dangerous amusement, are ingeni- ously managed, and give great life and interest to some parts of the work.

From **Unsigned notice, *Gentleman's Magazine***, vol. 86 (September 1816), pp. 248–9. Reprinted in *CH*, vol. I, p. 72

This reviewer is restrained in his praise of *Emma* and observes that it does not rank in the highest class of novels. Nevertheless, he also singles out the novel for its accurate depiction of 'the habits and manners of a middle class of gentry' rather than 'superior life'. The characters are praised, as are the unities of time and place. Like many of the early reviewers, he commends the book's humour.

Dulce est desipere in loco;[1] and a good Novel is now and then an agreeable relaxation from severer studies. Of this description was *Pride and Prejudice*; and from the entertainment which those volumes afforded us, we were desirous to peruse the present work; nor have our expectations been disappointed. If *Emma* has not the highly-drawn characters in superior life which are so interesting in *Pride and Prejudice*; it delineates with great accuracy the habits and the manners of a middle class of gentry; and of the inhabitants of a country village at one degree of rank and gentility beneath them. Every character throughout the work, from the heroine to the most subordinate, is a portrait which comes home to the heart and feelings of the Reader; who becomes familiarly acquainted with each of them, nor loses sight of a single individual till the completion of the work. The unities of time and place are well preserved; the language is chaste and correct; and if *Emma* be not allowed to rank in the very highest class of modern Novels, it certainly may claim at least a distinguished degree of eminence in that species of composition. It is amusing, if not instructive; and has no tendency to deteriorate the heart.

From **Charlotte Brontë on Jane Austen,** extract from letter to W. S. Williams, 12 April 1850. Reprinted in *CH*, vol. I, pp. 126–8

> Charlotte Brontë's correspondence with the critic George Henry Lewes and W. S. Williams (her publisher's reader for *Jane Eyre*) put forward the Romantic case against Jane Austen. As with Scott, Brontë employed a landscape analogy to express the differences in their art – but she turned the image to negative account, finding in Austen only 'a carefully fenced, highly cultivated garden, with neat borders and delicate flowers; but no glance of a bright, vivid physiognomy, no open country, no fresh air, no blue hill, no bonny beck'.[1] Having read *Emma*, she wrote to Williams and confirmed her lukewarm response in a comment that has dogged Austen criticism for decades: 'there is a Chinese fidelity, a miniature delicacy in the painting: she ruffles the reader by nothing vehement, disturbs him by nothing profound: the Passions are perfectly unknown to her'.

I have likewise read one of Miss Austen's works *Emma* – read it with interest and with just the degree of admiration which Miss Austen herself would have thought sensible and suitable – anything like warmth or enthusiasm; anything energetic, poignant, heartfelt, is utterly out of place in commending these works: all such demonstration the authoress would have met with a well-bred sneer, would have calmly scorned as outré and extravagant. She does her business of delineating the

---

1   'It is pleasant to indulge in trifles' (Horace, *Odes*, iv, 12, 28).

1   Not included as an extract – here Brontë was writing about *Pride and Prejudice* (see T. J. Wise and J. A. Symington, *The Brontës: Their Lives, Friendship and Correspondence* (Oxford: Blackwell, 1932)).

surface of the lives of genteel English people curiously well; there is a Chinese fidelity, a miniature delicacy in the painting: she ruffles her reader by nothing vehement, disturbs him by nothing profound: the Passions are perfectly unknown to her; she rejects even a speaking acquaintance with that stormy Sisterhood; even to the Feelings she vouchsafes no more than an occasional graceful but distant recognition; too frequent converse with them would ruffle the smooth elegance of her progress. Her business is not half so much with the human heart as with the human eyes, mouth, hands and feet; what sees keenly, speaks aptly, moves flexibly, it suits her to study, but what throbs fast and full, though hidden, what the blood rushes through, what is the unseen seat of Life and the sentient target of death – *this* Miss Austen ignores; she no more, with her mind's eye, beholds the heart of her race than each man, with bodily vision sees the heart in his heaving breast. Jane Austen was a complete and most sensible lady, but a very incomplete, and rather insensible (*not senseless*) woman, if this is heresy – I cannot help it.

From **George Henry Lewes, unsigned article, 'The Novels of Jane Austen'**, *Blackwood's Edinburgh Magazine* (July 1859), pp. 99–113. Reprinted *CH*, vol. I, pp. 148–66

The Victorian critic George Lewes (1817–78) was Austen's most fervent advocate in an age that had seen a dip in her popularity. This review is his final and most important appraisal of her work, which draws upon earlier pieces and acknowledges her superiority as a great artist. In an earlier review he had written: 'First and foremost let Jane Austen be named, the greatest artist that has ever written'. Lewes highly commends her 'economy of art' and the 'realism' of her characters: 'If ever living beings can be said to have moved across the page of fiction, as they lived, speaking as they spoke, and feeling as they felt, they do so in *Pride and Prejudice, Emma*, and *Mansfield Park*.' He compares her dramatic powers with those of Shakespeare, and praises her as a 'thorough mistress in the knowledge of human character'.

Nevertheless, picking up from Scott and Brontë, he acknowledges that her genius is limited: 'miniatures are not frescoes, and her works are miniatures'. One of the reasons for her neglect, he explains, is that, unlike George Eliot (Lewes's own common-law wife), she does not deliver the high art of the Victorians: 'she never stirs the deepest emotions . . . never fills the soul with a noble aspiration . . . only teaches us charity for the ordinary failings of ordinary people'.

If, as probably few will dispute, the art of the novelist be the representation of human life by means of a story; and if the *truest* representation, effected by the *least expenditure* of means, constitute the highest claim of art, then we say that Miss Austen has carried the art to a point of excellence surpassing that reached by any of her rivals . . . Miss Austen has nothing fervid in her works. She is not capable of producing a profound agitation in the mind. In many respects this is a limitation of her powers, a deduction from her claims. But while other writers have had more power over the emotions, more vivid imaginations, deeper sensibilities, deeper insight, and more of what is properly called invention, no novelist has approached her in what we may style the 'economy of art,' by which is meant the easy adaptation of means to ends, with no aid from extraneous or superfluous elements. . . . And if any one will examine the terms of the definition, he will perceive that almost all defects in works of art arise from neglect of this economy. When the *end* is the representation of human nature in its familiar aspects, moving amid every-day scenes, the *means* must likewise be furnished from every-day life: romance and improbabilities must be banished as rigorously as the grotesque exaggeration of peculiar characteristics, or the presentation of abstract types. It is easy for the artist to choose a subject from every-day life, but it is *not* easy for him so to represent the characters and their actions that they shall be at once lifelike and interesting; accordingly, whenever ordinary people are introduced, they are either made to speak a language never spoken out of books, and to pursue conduct never observed in life; or else they are intolerably wearisome. But Miss Austen is like Shakespeare: she makes her very noodles inexhaustibly amusing, yet accurately real. We never tire of her characters. They become equal to actual experiences. They live with us, and form perpetual topics of comment. We have so personal a dislike to Mrs Elton and Mrs Norris, that it would gratify our savage feeling to hear of some calamity befalling them. . . . Her reverend critic in the *Quarterly* truly says, 'She herself compares her productions to a little bit of ivory, two inches wide, worked upon with a brush so fine that little effect is produced with much labour. It is so: her portraits are perfect likenesses, admirably finished, many of them gems; but it is all miniature-painting; and having satisfied herself with being inimitable in one line, she never essayed canvass and oils; never tried her hand at a majestic daub'. . . . When we said that in the highest department of the novelist's art – namely, the truthful representation of character – Miss Austen was without a superior, we ought to have added that in this department she did not choose the highest range. . . . She belongs to the great dramatists; but her dramas are of homely common quality. [. . .]

[. . .] The secret is, Miss Austen was a thorough mistress in the knowledge of human character; how it is acted upon by education and circumstance, and how, when once formed, it shows itself through every hour of every day, and in every speech of every person. [. . .]

But the real secret of Miss Austen's success lies in her having the exquisite and rare gift of dramatic creation of character. [. . .] She seldom describes anything, and is not felicitous when she attempts it. But instead of *description*, the common and easy resource of novelists, she has the rare and difficult art of *dramatic presentation*: instead of telling us what her characters are, and what they feel, she presents the people, and they reveal themselves. In this she has never perhaps been surpassed, not even by Shakespeare himself. If ever living beings can be said to have moved across the page of fiction, as they lived, speaking as they spoke, and feeling as they felt, they do so in *Pride and Prejudice*, *Emma*, and *Mansfield Park*. [. . .]

[. . .] In what is commonly called 'plot' she does not excel. Her invention is wholly in character and motive, not in situation. Her materials are of the commonest every-day occurrence. Neither the emotions of tragedy, nor the exaggerations of farce, seem to have the slightest attraction for her. The reader's pulse never throbs, his curiosity is never intense; but his interest never wanes for a moment. The action begins; the people speak, feel, and act; everything that is said, felt, or done tends towards the entanglement or disentanglement of the plot; and we are almost made actors as well as spectators of the little drama. One of the most difficult things in dramatic writing is so to construct the story that every scene shall advance the denouement by easy evolution, yet at the same time give scope to the full exhibition of the characters. [. . .]

So entirely dramatic, and so little descriptive, is the genius of Miss Austen, that she seems to rely upon what her people say and do for the whole effect they are to produce on our imaginations. She no more thinks of describing the physical appearance of her people than the dramatist does who knows that his persons are to be represented by living actors. [. . .]

Her place is among great artists, but it is not high among them. She sits in the House of Peers, but it is as a simple Baron. The delight derived from her pictures arises from our sympathy with ordinary characters, our relish of humour, and our intellectual pleasure in art for art's sake. But when it is admitted that she never stirs the deeper emotions, that she never fills the soul with a noble aspiration, or brightens it with a fine idea, but, at the utmost, only teaches us charity for the ordinary failings of ordinary people, and sympathy with their goodness, we have admitted an objection which lowers her claims to rank among the great benefactors of the race; and this sufficiently explains why, with all her excellence, her name has not become a household word. Her fame, as we think, must endure. Such art as hers can never grow old, never be superseded. But, after all, miniatures are not frescoes, and her works are miniatures. Her place is among the Immortals; but the pedestal is erected in a quiet niche of the great temple.

From **Richard Simpson, unsigned review of the *Memoir*,** *North British Review,* vol. 52 (April 1870), pp. 129–52. Reprinted in *CH*, pp. 241–59

Richard Simpson (1820–76) was a Shakespearean scholar, an accomplished musicologist and a committed Roman Catholic (hence something of an outsider from the point of view of the Victorian cultural establishment). He wrote an extremely important review of Jane Austen, which paid full tribute to the force of her irony and her 'critical spirit'. His article presented a powerful counter-image to the 'dear Aunt Jane' of the 1870 *Memoir*. He saw that she was a serious, committed writer, who was interested in her craft, and whose artistic concerns were rooted in her early burlesques and satires. He regards her as an 'ironical censurer' who consciously rejected the 'poetic faculty' in favour of 'humour', 'delicacy of analysis' and 'subtlety of thought or language'. He also perceived her as an unsentimental realist, concerned with the moral improvement of her heroines. Before Simpson, critics praised Austen for her miniaturist portrayal of ordinary life. Simpson argued that, far from being limited, her 'little social commonwealths became a distinct personal entity to her imagination, with its own range of ideas, its own subject of discourse, its own public opinion on all social matters'. Despite this, he takes a predictable stance when he insists that she had no interest 'for the great political and social problems' of the day. This review went largely ignored, as the cult of gentle Jane mushroomed following the publication of the *Memoir*.

Although Miss Austen has left a great name in literature, she never belonged to the literary world. . . . She never aspired higher than to paint a system of four or five families revolving round a centre of attraction in a country mansion, or a lodging at Bath, or a house in a country town. This was, indeed, the only society she knew. Her name therefore, though great in a history of literature, counts for nothing in the history of men of letters. She stood by herself, and not only may but must be studied apart from them. [. . .]

It is clear that she began, as Shakespeare began, with being an ironical censurer of her contemporaries. After forming her prentice hand by writing nonsense, she began her artistic self-education by writing burlesques. One of her works, *Northanger Abbey*, still retains the traces and the flavour of these early essays. By it we may learn that her parodies were designed not so much to flout at the style as at the unnaturalness, unreality, and fictitious morality, of the romances she imitated. She began by being an ironical critic; she manifested her judgment of them not by direct censure, but by the indirect method of imitating and exaggerating the faults of her models, thus clearing the fountain by first stirring up the mud. This critical spirit lies at the foundation of her artistic faculty. Criticism, humour, irony, the judgment not of one that gives sentence but of the mimic who quizzes while he mocks, are her characteristics. [. . .]

[. . .] the paramount activity of the critical faculty is clearly seen in the didactic purpose . . . This didactic intention is even interwoven with the very plots and texture of the novel. The true hero, who at last secures the heroine's hand, is often a man sufficiently her elder to have been her guide and mentor in many of the most difficult crises of her youth. Miss Austen seems to be saturated with the Platonic idea that the giving and receiving of knowledge, the active formation of another's character, or the more passive growth under another's guidance, is the truest and strongest foundation of love. *Pride and Prejudice*, *Emma* and *Persuasion* all end with the heroes and heroines making comparisons of the intellectual and moral improvement which they have imparted to each other'. [. . .]

It is her thorough consciousness that man is a social being, and that apart from society there is not even the individual [. . .] she contemplates virtues, not as fixed quantities, or as definable qualities, but as continual struggles and conquests.

She defined her own sphere when she said that three or our families in a country village were the thing for a novelist to work upon. Each of these 'little social commonwealths' became a distinct personal entity to her imagination, with its own range of ideas, its own subject of discourse, its own public opinion on all social matters . . . She had no interest for the great political and social problems which were being debated with so much blood in her day. [. . .]

Her biographer refers to her fools as a class of characters in delineating which she has quite caught the knack of Shakespeare [. . .] In reality her fools are not more simple than her other characters. Her wisest personages have some dash of folly in them, and her least wise have something to love. [. . .] In the later novel, *Emma*, where perhaps Miss Austen perfects her processes for painting humour-ous portraits, the negative fool is much better represented in Miss Bates. Miss Bates has enough of womanly kindness and other qualities to make her a real living person, even a good Christian woman. But intellectually she is a negative fool. She has not mind enough to fall into contradictions [. . .] Mr Woodhouse [. . .] a mere white curd of asses' milk, but still a man with humanity enough in him to be loveable in spite of, nay partly because of, his weakness and foolishness.

Modern Criticism

From **Henry James, 'The Lesson of Balzac'**, *The Atlantic Monthly*, no. 96 (July 1905), pp. 166–80. Reprinted *CH*, vol. II, pp. 229–31

In 'The Lesson of Balzac', a lecture given in 1905, Henry James looked specifically at the novelist's reputation, and bemoaned the growth of the cosy, nostalgic and undiscriminating cult of Austen with its myth of the homely spinster writing for pleasure: 'our dear, everybody's dear, Jane'. It has nevertheless been a disappointment to critics that a writer so similar to Austen wrote so little about her. It is also striking that, unlike Simpson, James sees Austen as an instinctive artist who leaves us incurious 'of her process'.

Jane Austen, with all her light felicity, leaves us hardly more curious of her process, or of the experience in her that fed it, than the brown thrush who tells his story from the garden bough; and this, I freely confess, in spite of her being one of those of the shelved and safe, for all time, of whom I should have liked to begin by talking; one of those in whose favor discrimination has long since practically operated. She is in fact a signal instance of the way it does, with all its embarrassments, at last infallibly operate. A sharp short cut, one of the sharpest and shortest achieved, in this field, by the general judgment, came out, betimes, straight at her feet. Practically overlooked for thirty or forty years after her death, she perhaps really stands there for us as the prettiest possible example of that rectification of estimate, brought about by some slow clearance of stupidity, the half-century or so is capable of working round to. This tide has risen high on the opposite shore, the shore of appreciation – risen rather higher, I think, than the high-water mark, the highest, of her intrinsic merit and interest; though I grant indeed – as a point to be made – that we are dealing here in some degree with the tides so freely driven up, beyond their mere logical reach, by the stiff breeze of the commercial, in other words of the special bookselling spirit; an eager, active, interfering force which has a great many confusions of apparent value, a great many wild and. wandering estimates, to answer for. For these distinctively mechanical and overdone reactions, of course, the critical spirit, even in its most relaxed mood, is not responsible. Responsible, rather, is the body of publishers, editors, illustrators, producers of the pleasant twaddle of magazines; who have found their 'dear,' our dear, everybody's dear, Jane so infinitely to their material purpose, so amenable to pretty reproduction in every variety of what is called tasteful, and in what seemingly proves to be saleable, form.

[. . .] The key to Jane Austen's fortune with posterity has been in part the extraordinary grace of her facility, in fact of her unconsciousness: as if, at the most, for difficulty, for embarrassment, she sometimes, over her work-basket, her tapestry flowers, in the spare, cool drawing-room of other days, fell a-musing, lapsed too metaphorically, as one may say, into wool-gathering, and her dropped stitches, of these pardonable, of these precious moments, were afterwards picked up as little touches of human truth, little glimpses of steady vision, little master-strokes of imagination.

From **A. C. Bradley, 'Jane Austen'**, a lecture first given at Newnham College, Cambridge, in 1911; final text printed in *Essays and Studies*, vol. 2 (1911), pp. 7–36. Reprinted *CH*, vol. II, pp. 233–8

A. C. Bradley, most famous for his Oxford University lectures on *Shakespearean Tragedy*, names *Emma* as the best of the novels and traces the influence of Dr Johnson on Austen. He describes Austen as a moralist and a humorist. As often, Miss Bates and Mr Woodhouse are singled out as comic creations who inspire affection in the reader.

There are two distinct strains in Jane Austen. She is a moralist and a humorist. These strains are often blended or even completely fused, but still they may be distinguished. It is the first that connects her with Johnson, by whom, I suspect, she was a good deal influenced. With an intellect much less massive, she still observes human nature with the same penetration and the same complete honesty. . . . We remember Johnson in those passages where she refuses to express a deeper concern than she feels for misfortune or grief, and with both there is an occasional touch of brutality in the manner of the refusal. It is a question, however, of manner alone, and when she speaks her mind fully and gravely she speaks for Johnson too; as when she makes Emma say: 'I hope it may be allowed that, if compassion has produced exertion and relief to the sufferers, it has done all that is truly important. If we feel for the wretched enough to do all we can for them, the rest is empty sympathy, only distressing to ourselves'. Finally, like Johnson, she is, in the strict sense, a moralist. Her morality, that is to say, is not merely embodied in her plots, it is often openly expressed. [. . .]

But Jane Austen's favourite attitude, we may even say her instinctive attitude, is, of course, that of the humorist. And this is not all. The foibles, illusions, self-contradictions, of human nature are a joy to her for their own sakes, but also because through action they lead to consequences which may be serious but may also be comic. In that case they produce sometimes matter fit for a comedy, a play in which people's lives fall into an entanglement of errors, misunderstandings, and cross-purposes, from which they are rescued, not by their own wisdom or skill, but by the kindness of Fortune or some Providence with a weakness for lovers.

[. . .] She is never cynical, and not often merely satirical. A cynic or a mere satirist may be intellectually pleased by human absurdities and illusions, but he does not feel them to be good. But to Jane Austen, so far as they are not seriously harmful, they are altogether pleasant, because they are both ridiculous and right. It is amusing, for example, that Knightley, who is almost a model of good sense, right feeling, and just action, should be unjust to Frank Churchill because, though he does not know it, he himself is in love with Emma: but to Jane Austen that is not only the way a man *is* made, but the way he *should* be made. No doubt there are plenty of things that should not be, but when we so regard them they are not comical. A main point of difference between Jane Austen and Johnson is that to her much of the world is amusing, and much more of it is right. She is less of a moralist and more of a humorist.

Emma is the most vivacious of the later novels, and with some readers the first favourite. In plot-interest it is probably the strongest of the six, and, not to speak of the more prominent persons, it contains, in Mr Woodhouse and Miss Bates, two minor characters who resemble one another in being the object equally of our laughter and our unqualified respect and affection. [. . .]

Emma is satisfactory on the more serious side of the story; but I will not dwell on that. In its main design it is a comedy, and, as a comedy, unsurpassed, I think, among novels, and all the better because Jane Austen does not affront us like Meredith in *The Egoist*,[1] by coming forward as interpreter. Most of the characters are involved in the contrast of reality and illusion, but it is concentrated on Emma. This young lady, who is always surpassingly confident of being right, is always surpassingly wrong. She is reputed very clever, and she *is* clever; and she never sees the fact and never understands herself. A spoiled child, with a good disposition and more will than most of the people in her little world, she begins to put this world to rights. She chooses for a friend, not Jane Fairfax her equal, but the amiable, soft, stupid, and adoring Harriet Smith. Her motive, which she supposes to be kindness, is the pleasure of patronage and management. She detaches Harriet's affections from a suitable lover, and fastens them on a person wholly unsuitable and perfectly indifferent. [. . .] In a sketch like this the comedy of the story loses both its fun and its verisimilitude, but we know how delightful it is, and on the whole how true to human nature. Though we may not care for *Emma* most, I think the claim may fairly be made for it that, of all the novels, it most perfectly executes its design.

---

1   *The Egoist* (1879), a much-admired late Victorian novel by George Meredith, who wrote with a highly distinctive and stylized authorial voice.

From **Reginald Farrer, 'Jane Austen, *ob.* July 18, 1817'**, *Quarterly Review*, July 1917. Reprinted *CH*, vol. II, pp. 245–71

The year 1917 marked the centenary of Jane Austen's death. Reginald Farrer's seminal essay was printed in the same year, in one of the leading literary periodicals of this age of public criticism. This was a significant review in which *Emma* was described as the 'Book of Books'. Farrer anticipates the formalism or new criticism of the mid-twentieth century in his emphasis on the technical mastery of *Emma*. The difficulty for Austen in creating a heroine such as Emma is that she must balance sympathetic identification with critical detachment; she must be both inside and outside her main character. Farrer reminds the reader that Emma is a comic figure who is 'never to be taken seriously', and 'it is only those who have not realized this who will be "put off" by her absurdities, her snobberies, her misdirected mischievous ingenuities.'

But now we come to the Book of Books, which is the book of Emma Woodhouse. And justly so named, with Jane Austen's undeviating flair for the exact title. For the whole thing *is* Emma; there is only one short scene in which Emma herself is not on the stage; and that one scene is Knightley's conversation about her with Mrs Weston. Take it all in all, *Emma* is the very climax of Jane Austen's work; and a real appreciation of *Emma* is the final test of citizenship in her kingdom. For this is not an easy book to read; it should never be the beginner's primer, nor be published without a prefatory synopsis. Only when the story has been thoroughly assimilated, can the infinite delights and subtleties of its workmanship begin to be appreciated, as you realize the manifold complexity of the book's web, and find that every sentence, almost every epithet, has its definite reference to equally unemphasised points before and after in the development of the plot. Thus it is that, while twelve readings of *Pride and Prejudice* give you twelve periods of pleasure repeated, as many readings of *Emma* give you that pleasure, not repeated only, but squared and squared again with each perusal, till at every fresh reading you feel anew that you never understood anything like the widening sum of its delights. But, until you know the story, you are apt to find its movement dense and slow and obscure, difficult to follow, and not very obviously worth the following.

For this is *the* novel of character, and of character alone, and of one dominating character in particular. And many a rash reader, and some who are not rash, have been shut out on the threshold of Emma's Comedy by a dislike of Emma herself. Well did Jane Austen know what she was about, when she said, 'I am going to take a heroine whom nobody but myself will much like.' And, in so far as she fails to make people like Emma, so far would her whole attempt have to be judged a failure, were it not that really the failure, like the loss, is theirs who have not taken the trouble to understand what is being attempted. Jane Austen loved tackling problems; her hardest of all, her most deliberate, and her most triumphantly solved, is Emma.

What is that problem? No one who carefully reads the first three opening paragraphs of the book can entertain a doubt, or need any prefatory synopsis; for in these the author gives us quite clear warning of what we are to see. We are to see the gradual humiliation of self-conceit, through a long self-wrought succession of disasters, serious in effect, but keyed in Comedy throughout. Emma herself, in fact, *is never to be taken seriously*. And it is only those who have not realized this who will be 'put off' by her absurdities, her snobberies, her misdirected mischievous ingenuities. Emma is simply a figure of fun. To conciliate affection for a character, not because of its charms, but in defiance of its defects, is the loftiest aim of the comic spirit; Shakespeare achieved it with his besotted old rogue of a Falstaff, and Molière with Celimène. It is with these, not with 'sympathetic' heroines, that Emma takes rank, as the culminating figure of English high-comedy. And to attain success in creating a being whom you both love and laugh at, the author must attempt a task of complicated difficulty. He must both run with the hare and hunt with the hounds, treat his creation at once objectively and subjectively, get inside it to inspire it with sympathy, and yet stay outside it to direct laughter on its comic aspects. And this is what Jane Austen does for Emma, with a consistent sublimity so demure that indeed a reader accustomed only to crude work might be pardoned for missing the point of her innumerable hints, and actually taking seriously, for example, the irony with which Emma's attitude about the Coles' dinner-party is treated, or the even more convulsing comedy of Emma's reflexions after it. But only Jane Austen is capable of such oblique glints of humour; and only in *Emma* does she weave them so densely into her kaleidoscope that the reader must be perpetually on his guard lest some specially delicious flash escape his notice, or some touch of dialogue be taken for the author's own intention.

Yet, as Emma really does behave extremely ill by Jane Fairfax, and even worse by Robert Martin, merely to laugh would not be enough, and every disapproval would justly be deepened to dislike. But, when we realize that each machination of Emma's, each imagined piece of penetration, is to be a thread in the snare woven unconsciously by herself for her own enmeshing in disaster, then the balance is rectified again, and disapproval can lighten to laughter once more. For this is another of Jane Austen's triumphs here – the way in which she keeps our sympathies poised about Emma. [. . .]

[. . .] *Emma* contains no fewer than four silly people, more or less prominent in the story; but Jane Austen touches them all with a new mansuetude, and turns them out as candidates for love as well as laughter. Nor is this all that must be said for Miss Bates and Mr Woodhouse. They are actually inspired with sympathy. Specially remarkable is the treatment of Miss Bates, whose pathos depends on her lovableness, and her lovableness on her pathos, till she comes so near our hearts that Emma's abrupt brutality to her on Box Hill comes home to us with the actuality of a violent sudden slap in our own face. But then Miss Bates, though a twaddle, is by no means a fool; in her humble, quiet, unassuming happiness, she is shown throughout as an essentially wise woman.

From **D. W. Harding, 'Regulated Hatred: An Aspect of the Work of Jane Austen'**, *Scrutiny*, vol. 8 (March 1940), pp. 346–62 (Cambridge: Cambridge University Press)

D. W. Harding was a psychologist as well as a literary critic. His article has had a profound impact on Austen criticism. Harding describes Austen as a subversive author, hostile to her environment, whose writing was her way 'of finding some mode of existence for her critical attitudes'. Her 'hatred' is so 'regulated' that most readers fail to see it, and her books 'read and enjoyed by precisely the sort of people whom she disliked'. Harding's psychoanalytical view of Austen's suppression and displacement was not initially popular amongst the more genteel readers of the 1940s and 1950s, but it was vitally important in shaking off the complacency of the view of her as a comfortable and uncritical writer. Other writers also began to seen her as subversive.

In *Emma* . . . Jane Austen seems to be on perfectly good terms with the public she is addressing and to have no reserve in offering the funniness and virtues of Mr Woodhouse and Miss Bates to be judged by the accepted standards of the public. She invites her readers to be just their natural patronising selves. But this public that Jane Austen seems on such good terms with has some curious things said about it, not criticisms, but small notes of fact that are usually not made. They almost certainly go unnoticed by many readers, for they involve only the faintest change of tone from something much more usual and acceptable.

When she says that Miss Bates 'enjoyed a most uncommon degree of popularity for a woman neither young, handsome, rich, nor married', this is fairly conventional satire that any reading public would cheerfully admit in its satirist and chuckle over. But the next sentence must have to be mentally rewritten by the greater number of Jane Austen's readers. For them it probably runs, 'Miss Bates stood in the very worst predicament in the world for having much of the public favour; and she had no intellectual superiority to make atonement to herself, or compel an outward respect from those who might despise her.' This, I suggest, is how most readers, lulled and disarmed by the amiable context, will soften what in fact reads, '. . . and she had no intellectual superiority to make atonement to herself, or frighten those who might hate her into outward respect'. Jane Austen was herself at this time 'neither young, handsome, rich, nor married', and the passage perhaps hints at the functions which her unquestioned intellectual superiority may have had for her.

This eruption of fear and hatred into the relationships of everyday social life is something that the urbane admirer of Jane Austen finds distasteful; it is not the satire of one who writes securely for the entertainment of her civilised acquaintances. And it has the effect, for the attentive reader, of changing the flavour of the more ordinary satire amongst which it is embedded. [. . .]

[. . .] But in *Emma* the style changes: the talk at the Coles' dinner party, a pleasant dinner party which the heroine enjoyed, is described as '. . . the usual rate of conversation; a few clever things said, a few downright silly, but by much the larger proportion neither the one nor the other – nothing worse than everyday remarks, dull repetitions, old news, and heavy jokes'. 'Nothing worse'! – that phrase is typical. It is not mere sarcasm by any means. Jane Austen genuinely valued the achievements of the civilisation she lived within and never lost sight of the fact that there might be something vastly worse than the conversation she referred to. 'Nothing worse' is a positive tribute to the decency, the superficial friendliness, the absence of the grosser forms of insolence and self-display at the dinner party. At least Mrs Elton wasn't there. And yet the effect of the comment, if her readers took it seriously would be that of a disintegrating attack upon the sort of social intercourse they have established for themselves. It is not the comment of one who would have helped to make her society what it was, or ours what it is.

To speak of this aspect of her work as 'satire' is perhaps misleading. She has none of the underlying didactic intention ordinarily attributed to the satirist. Her object is not missionary; it is the more desperate one of merely finding some mode of existence for her critical attitudes. To her the first necessity was to keep on reasonably good terms with the associates of her everyday life; she had a deep need of their affection and a genuine respect for the ordered, decent civilisation that they upheld. And yet she was sensitive to their crudenesses and complacencies and knew that her real existence depended on resisting many of the values they implied. The novels gave her a way out of this dilemma. This, rather than the ambition of entertaining a posterity of urbane gentlemen, was her motive force in writing. [. . .]

[In *Emma*] the underlying argument has a different trend. She continues to see that the heroine has derived from the people and conditions around her, but she now keeps clearly in mind the objectionable features of those people; and she faces the far bolder conclusion that even a heroine is likely to have assimilated many of the more unpleasant possibilities of the human being in society.

From **Edmund Wilson, 'A Long Talk about Jane Austen'** (1945), in Ian Watt, ed., *Jane Austen: A Collection of Critical Essays* (Englewood Cliffs, NJ: Prentice-Hall, 1963), pp. 35–40, repr. from *Classics and Commercials: A Literary Chronicle of the Forties* by Edmund Wilson (New York: Farrar, Straus, 1950)

The New York writer Edmund Wilson was the first to suggest that Emma herself is more interested in women than men. Emma's sexuality has continued to be pondered by critics, though, unlike some later critics, Wilson is not censorious about what might be perceived as Emma's semi-repressed homosexuality – he even suggests that at the end of the novel Emma will set up a ménage à trois consisting of herself, Mr Knightley and a Harriet Smith substitute. His views on Emma's lesbianism and on the emasculating of Mr Woodhouse, a 'silly old woman', were taken up and more consciously politicized by feminist and gender-oriented critics later in the century. Wilson's sense of the diversity of possible approaches to the novel still holds good, as critics continue to disagree with one another in their readings of it.

Emma . . . is with Jane Austen what *Hamlet* is with Shakespeare. It is the book of hers about which her readers are likely to disagree most; they tend either to praise it extravagantly or to find it dull, formless, and puzzling. The reason for this, I believe, is that, just as in the case of *Hamlet*, there is something outside the picture which is never made explicit in the story but which has to be recognized by the reader before it is possible for him to appreciate the book. Many women readers feel instinctively the psychological rightness of the behavior attributed to Emma, and they are the ones who admire the novel. Some male readers, like Justice Holmes,[1] who was certainly a connoisseur of fiction yet who wrote to Sir Frederick Pollock that, 'bar Miss Bates,' he was 'bored by *Emma*,' never succeed in getting into the story because they cannot see what it is all about. Why does Emma take up her two protégées? Why does she become so much obsessed by her plans for them? Why does she mistake the realities so and go so ludicrously wrong about them? Why does it take her so unconscionably long to reach the obvious rapprochement with Knightley?

The answer is that Emma is not interested in men except in the paternal relation. Her actual father is a silly old woman: in their household it is Emma herself who, motherless as she is, assumes the functions of head of the family; it is she who takes the place of the parent and Mr Woodhouse who becomes the child. It is Knightley who has checked and rebuked her, who has presided over her social development, and she accepts him as a substitute father; she finally marries him and brings him into her own household, where his role is to reinforce Mr Woodhouse. Miss Stern sees the difficulties of this odd situation. 'Oh, Miss Austen,' she cries, 'it was *not* a good solution; it was a bad solution, an unhappy ending, could we see beyond the last pages of the book.' But among the contretemps she foresees she does not mention what would surely have been the worst. Emma, who was relatively indifferent to men, was inclined to infatuations with women; and what reason is there to believe that her marriage with Knightley would prevent her from going on as she had done before: from discovering a new young lady as appealing as Harriet Smith, dominating her personality and situating her in a dream-world of Emma's own in which Emma would be able to confer on her all kinds of imaginary benefits but which would have no connection whatever with her condition or her real possibilities? This would worry and exasperate Knightley and be hard for him to do anything about. He would be lucky if he did not presently find himself saddled, along with the other awkward features of the arrangement, with one of Emma's young protégées as an actual member of the household.

---

1   Oliver Wendell Holmes (1809–94), influential New England (Harvard) intellectual and man of letters of the late nineteenth century.

From **F. R. Leavis, *The Great Tradition*** (London: Chatto & Windus, 1948, reprinted 1962), pp. 5–8

> The Cambridge University critic F. R. Leavis's *The Great Tradition* (1948) was one of the most influential books of the period. Though the book was mainly concerned with George Eliot, Henry James and Joseph Conrad, Leavis placed Austen at the very forefront of his 'great tradition' of English novelists. As well as emphasizing her 'formal perfection', he drew attention to her 'marked moral intensity'.

Jane Austen's plots, and her novels in general, were put together very 'deliberately and calculatedly' (if not 'like a building'). But her interest in 'composition' is not something to be put over against her interest in life; nor does she offer an 'aesthetic' value that is separable from moral significance. The principle of organization, and the principle of development, in her work is an intense moral interest of her own in life that is in the first place a preoccupation with certain problems that life compels on her as personal ones. She is intelligent and serious enough to be able to impersonalize her moral tensions as she strives, in her art, to become more fully conscious of them, and to learn what, in the interests of life, she ought to do with them. Without her intense moral preoccupation she wouldn't have been a great novelist.

[. . .] Jane Austen, in fact, is the inaugurator of the great tradition of the English novel – and by 'great tradition' I mean the tradition to which what is great in English fiction belongs. [. . .]

As a matter of fact, when we examine the formal perfection of *Emma*, we find that it can be appreciated only in terms of the moral preoccupations that characterize the novelist's peculiar interest in life. Those who suppose it to be an 'aesthetic matter', a beauty of 'composition' that is combined, miraculously, with 'truth to life', can give no adequate reason for the view that *Emma* is a great novel, and no intelligent account of its perfection of form.

From **Arnold Kettle, 'Jane Austen: *Emma*'**, from *An Introduction to the English Novel* (London: Hutchinson Publishing Group, 1951). Reprinted in David Lodge, ed., *Emma: A Casebook* (London and Basingstoke: Macmillan Press, 1975), pp. 89–103

> Arnold Kettle was a pioneering Marxist literary critic of an earlier generation than the newly politicized critics who emerged in the 1970s and 1980s: his essay anticipates many of the issues raised by later ideologically oriented critics.

The silliest of all criticisms of Jane Austen is the one which blames her for not writing about the Battle of Waterloo and the French Revolution. She wrote about what she understood and no artist can do more.

But did she understand enough? The question is not a silly one, for it must be recognized that her world was not merely small but narrow. Her novels are some- times referred to as miniatures, but the analogy is not apt. We do not get from *Emma* a condensed and refined sense of a larger entity. Neither is it a symbolic work suggesting references far beyond its surface meaning. The limitations of the Highbury world, which are indeed those of Surrey in about 1814, are likely therefore to be reflected in the total impact of the novel.

The limitation and the narrowness of the Highbury world is the limitation of class society. And the one important criticism of Jane Austen (we will suspend judgment for the moment on its truth) is that her vision is limited by her unquestioning acceptance of class society. That she did not write about the French Revolution or the Industrial Revolution is as irrelevant as that she did not write about the Holy Roman Empire; they were not her subjects. But Highbury is her subject and no sensitive contemporary reader can fail to sense here an inadequacy (again, we will suspend judgment on its validity). It is necessary to insist, at this point, that the question at issue is not Jane Austen's failure to suggest a *solution* to the problem of class divisions but her apparent failure to notice the *existence* of the problem.

The values and standards of the Highbury world are based on the assumption that it is right and proper for a minority of the community to live at the expense of the majority. No amount of sophistry can get away from this fact and to discuss the moral concern of Jane Austen without facing it would be hypocrisy. It is perfectly true that, within the assumptions of aristocratic society, the values recommended in *Emma* are sensitive enough. Snobbery, smugness, condescen- sion, lack of consideration, unkindness of any description, are held up to our disdain. But the fundamental condescension, the basic unkindness which permits the sensitive values of *Emma* to be applicable only to one person in ten or twenty, is this not left unscathed? Is there not here a complacency which renders the hundred little incomplacencies almost irrelevant?

From **Marvin Mudrick, 'Irony as Form: *Emma*'**, in his *Jane Austen: Irony as Defense and Discovery* (Princeton, NJ: Princeton University Press, 1952; reprinted 1974), pp. 181–206

The American critic Marvin Mudrick followed both Harding and Wilson in his views of Austen as a subversive writer. He argued that irony was her 'means of defense and discovery' and, like Wilson, he found intimations of lesbian desire in Emma's infatuation with Harriet. Mudrick suggests that Emma is an unpleasant heroine who is incapable of committing herself 'humanly'. He contentiously argues that Emma's supposed reformation is the ultimate irony of a novel that is steeped in irony: 'The irony of *Emma* is multiple; and its ultimate aspect is that there is no happy ending'.

Emma observes Harriet's beauty with far more warmth than anyone else: 'She was so busy in admiring those soft blue eyes, in talking and listening, and forming all these schemes in the in-betweens, that the evening flew away at a very unusual rate'. This is the clever and sophisticated Emma, transported by the presence of the most insipid girl imaginable. Moreover, Emma's attention never falls so warmly upon a man; against this feeling for Harriet, her good words for Mr Knightley's appearance seem pale indeed. [. . .]

No one, it seems, is attracted by *this* pretty face except Emma. [. . .]

The fact is that Emma prefers the company of women, more particularly of women whom she can master and direct; the fact is that this preference is intrinsic to her whole dominating and uncommitting personality. [. . .]

Emma needs to dominate, she can of course – in her class and time – most easily dominate women; and her need is urgent enough to forgo even the pretense of sympathetic understanding. She feels affection only towards Harriet, Mrs Weston, and her father: instances, not of tenderness, but rather of satisfied control. She feels affection only toward those immediately under her command, and all of them are women. [. . .]

Emma plays God because she cannot commit herself humanly. Her compulsion operates in the absence of one quality: a quality which Emma, Frank Churchill, and Mrs Elton – the only destructive figures in the novel – are all without. The quality is tenderness. For Emma, there is no communication of feeling. She can esteem, loathe, praise, censure, grieve, rejoice – but she cannot feel like anyone else in the world. Her ego will admit nothing but itself. [. . .]

The primary large irony of the novel is, then, the deceptiveness of surface. Charm is the chief warning-signal of Jane Austen's world, for it is most often the signal of wit adrift from feeling. The brilliant façades of Emma and Frank Churchill have no door. [. . .]

When we first observe Emma's maneuverings with Harriet, it is with the consciousness of her urge to dominate. Soon, though, this urge has become inextricable from Emma's own snobbery and her vicarious snobbery for Harriet, which drive it even farther from the possibility of caution or rational direction. Why does Emma want Harriet to marry? Harriet begins to seem a kind of proxy for Emma, a means by which Emma – too reluctant, too fearful of involvement, to consider the attempt herself – may discover what marriage is like. If Harriet is a proxy for Emma, she must serve as a defense also. Emma is outraged by Mr Elton's proposal, not merely because she has not expected it (the basis of the simple irony here), but because Mr Elton dares to circumvent the buffer she has so carefully set up. Harriet is to experience for her what she refuses to commit herself to, but cannot help being curious about. Yet Harriet is a very pretty girl, and being infinitely stupid and unperceptive, may be used in other uncommitting ways. Emma's interest in Harriet is not merely mistress-and-pupil, but quite emotional and particular: for a time at least – until Harriet becomes slightly resentful of the yoke after Emma's repeated blunders – Emma is in love with her: a love unphysical and inadmissible, even perhaps undefinable in such a society; and therefore safe. And in all this web of relations, by no means exhausted here, we return always to Emma's over-powering motive: her fear of commitment. [. . .]

[. . .] Emma has finally – almost – got to know herself; but only because the knowledge is here painless and may be discarded in a little while with Mr Knightley again, where she may resume, however self-amusedly for the present, her characteristic role:

'Do you dare say this?' cried Mr Knightley. 'Do you dare to suppose me so great a blockhead, as not to know what a man is talking of? – What do you deserve?'
'Oh! I always deserve the best treatment, because I never put up with any other . . .'

[. . .] The irony of *Emma* is multiple; and its ultimate aspect is that there is no happy ending, easy equilibrium, if we care to project confirmed exploiters like Emma and Churchill into the future of their marriages.

From **Lionel Trilling, '*Emma* and the Legend of Jane Austen'** (1957), in his *Beyond Culture: Essays on Literature and Learning* (New York: Viking, 1965), pp. 31–55

> The influential American critic Lionel Trilling gives a 'liberal humanist' reading of *Emma* which bears some resemblances to Leavis's moral criticism, albeit in a more relaxed and urbane tone: 'To represent the possibility of controlling the personal life, of becoming acquainted with ourselves, of creating a community of "intelligent love" – this is indeed to make an extraordinary promise and to hold out a rare hope.' Trilling sees the novel as a pastoral 'idyll' to be considered apart from the real world, with Mr Woodhouse and Miss Bates as 'Holy fools'. But paradoxically, he argues that this most English of novels is 'touched by national feeling'. Emma's gravest error is to separate Harriet Smith from Robert Martin, 'a mistake of nothing less of national import'. Some of Trilling's assumptions are distinctive of his age and class (liberal, well-to-do Manhattan intellectual life of the immediate post-war era) – the extract begins with an assumption that many later twentieth-century critics would regard as cringingly sexist – but his good judgment and intelligence as a reader, together with his unbending commitment to the serious importance of literature – shine through.

The extraordinary thing about Emma is that she has a moral life as a man has a moral life. And she doesn't have it as a special instance, as an example of a new kind of woman, which is the way George Eliot's Dorothea Brooke has her moral life, but quite as a matter of course, as a given quality of her nature. [. . .]

Inevitably we are drawn to Emma. But inevitably we hold her to be deeply at fault. Her self-love leads her to be a self-deceiver. She can be unkind. She is a dreadful snob.

[. . .] But when Emma presumes to look down on the young farmer, Robert Martin, and undertakes to keep little Harriet Smith from marrying him, she makes a truly serious mistake, a mistake of nothing less than national import.

Here it is to be observed that *Emma* is a novel that is touched – lightly but indubitably – by national feeling. . . . At any rate, there appears in *Emma* a tendency to conceive of a specifically English ideal of life. Knightley speaks of Frank Churchill as falling short of the demands of this ideal: 'No, Emma, your amiable young man can be amiable only in French, not in English. He may be very "aimable", have very good manners, and be very agreeable; but he can have no English delicacy towards the feelings of other people: nothing really amiable about him.' Again, in a curiously impressive moment in the book, we are given a detailed description of the countryside as seen by the party at Donwell Abbey, and this comment follows: 'It was a sweet view – sweet to the eye and the mind. English verdure, English culture [agriculture, of course, is meant], English comfort, seen under a sun bright without being oppressive.' This is a larger consideration than the occasion would appear to require; there seems no reason to expect this vision of 'England's green and pleasant land'. Or none until we note that the description of the view closes thus: '. . . and at the bottom of this bank, favourably placed and sheltered, rose the Abbey-Mill Farm, with meadows in front, and the river making a close and handsome curve around it'. Abbey-Mill Farm is the property of young Robert Martin, for whom Emma has expressed a principled social contempt, and the little burst of strong feeling has the effect, among others, of pointing up the extremity of Emma's mistake. [. . .]

Emma's snobbery, then, is nothing less than a contravention of the best – and safest – tendency of English social life. [. . .]

[. . .] And in the community of Highbury, Miss Bates and Mr Woodhouse are sacred. They are fools, to be sure, as everyone knows. But they are fools of a special and transcendent kind. They are innocents – of such is the kingdom of heaven. They are children, who have learned nothing of the guile of the world. And their mode of existence is the key to the nature of the world of Highbury, which is the world of the pastoral idyll. [. . .]

The impulse to believe that the world of Jane Austen really did exist leads to notable error. 'Jane Austen's England' is the thoughtless phrase which is often made to stand for the England of the years in which our author lived, although any serious history will make it sufficiently clear that the England of her novels was not the real England, except as it gave her the license to imagine the England which we call hers. This England, especially as it is represented in *Emma*, is an idyll. The error of identifying it with the actual England ought always to be remarked. Yet the same sense of actuality that corrects the error should not fail to recognize the remarkable force of the ideal that leads many to make the error. To represent the possibility of controlling the personal life, of becoming acquainted with ourselves, of creating a community of 'intelligent love' – this is indeed to make an extraordinary promise and to hold out a rare hope. We ought not be shocked and repelled if some among us think there really was a time when such promises and hopes were realized. Nor ought we be entirely surprised if, when they speak of the person who makes such promises and holds out such hopes, they represent her as not merely a novelist, if they find it natural to deal with her as a figure of legend and myth.

From **Mark Schorer, 'The Humiliation of Emma Woodhouse'**
(1959), in Ian Watt, ed., *Jane Austen: A Collection of Critical Essays* (Englewood Cliffs, NJ: Prentice-Hall, 1963), pp. 98–111, reprinted from *The Literary Review* (Teaneck, NJ: Farleigh Dickinson University), vol. II, no. 4 (Summer 1959), pp. 547–63

Mark Schorer considers the novel by closely analysing its verbal and linguistic patterns. He argues that Austen's language is steeped in metaphors drawn from 'commerce and property', and that she depicts a world of 'peculiarly material values', which is ironically juxtaposed with her depiction of 'moral propriety'. Austen's 'moral realism' is concerned with the adjustments made between material and moral values. Emma must drop in the social scale to rise in the moral scale. Schorer's contention that Emma must be punished and humiliated has been condemned by later feminist critics as representative of the 'Girl being taught a lesson' mode of Austenian criticism (see **p. 85**).

Jane Austen's *Emma*, 1816, stands at the head of her achievements, and, even though she herself spoke of Emma as 'a heroine whom no one but myself will much like', discriminating readers have thought the novel her greatest. Her powers here are at their fullest, her control at its most certain. As with most of her novels, it has a double theme, but in no other has the structure been raised so skillfully upon it. . . . No novel shows more clearly Jane Austen's power to take the moral measurement of the society with which she was concerned through the range of her characters. [. . .]

[. . .] Jane Austen's style is, of course, remarkably nonmetaphorical, if we are thinking of explicit metaphor, the stated analogy, but it is no less remarkable in the persistency with which the buried or dead metaphors in her prose imply one consistent set of values. These are the values of commerce and property, of the counting house and the inherited estate. I will divide this set of values rather arbitrarily into five categories. First of all, of *scale* itself, all that metaphor of high and low, sink and rise, advance and decline, superior and inferior, rank and fortune, power and command; as 'held below the level', 'raise her expectations too high', 'materially cast down', 'the intimacy between her and Emma must sink'. Second, of *money*: credit, value, interest, rate, reserve, secure, change and exchange, alloy, resources, gain, want, collect (for 'assume'), reckon, render, account, claim, profit, loss, accrue, tax, due, pay, lose, spend, waste, fluctuate, dispense, 'precious deposit', appropriate, commission, safety. Third, of *business and property*: inherit, certify, procure, solicit, entitle, business, venture, scheme, arrangement, insure, cut off, trust, charge, stock. Fourth, of *number and measure*: add, divide, multiply, calculate, how much and how little, more and less. And fifth, of *matter*: incumbrance, weight, substance, material (as, material change, or material alteration), comfort.

These terms are constantly appearing, both singly and in clusters. One or two illustrations must suffice:

> She listened, and found it well *worth* listening to. That very *dear* part of Emma, her fancy, *received* an amusing *supply* . . . it became henceforth her *prime object of interest*; and during the ten days of their stay at Hartfield it was not to be expected – she did not herself expect – that anything beyond occasional fortuitous assistance could be *afforded by her* to the lovers. They *might advance* rapidly if they would, however; they *must advance* somehow or other, whether they would or no. She hardly wished to have more leisure for them. They are people, who *the more you do* for them, *the less they will do* for themselves. Mr and Mrs John Knightley . . . were exciting, of course, rather *more than the usual interest.* Till this year, every long vacation since their marriage had been *divided* between Hartfield and Donwell Abbey. [emphasis Shorer's]

[. . .] It would seem that we are in a world of peculiarly *material* value, a world of almost instinctive material interests in its basic, intuitive response to experience. The style has created a texture, the 'special feel' of that world. At the same time, on the surface of the action, this is usually a world of refined sensibility, of concern with moral propriety, and in Emma's case, presumably at least, of intelligent clarity of evaluation. A large portion of Jane Austen's comedy arises from the discrepancy that we see here, from the tension between these two kinds of value, these different *scales*, material and moral, which the characters, like the metaphors, are all the time juxtaposing and equating. But when we say that, we have moved from considerations of language alone, into the function of the language in the whole. [. . .]

[. . .] The texture of the style itself announces, therefore, the subject, and warns us, suggesting that we not be deceived by the fine sentiments and the moral scruples of the surface; that this is a material world where property and rank are major and probably as important as 'characters'. More specifically, that this is not simply a novel of courtship and marriage, but a novel about the economic and social significance of courtship and marriage. (The basic situation in all the novels arises from the economics of marriage.) [. . .]

. . . For all her superiority, Emma's values are really the values of the society she patronizes. [. . .]

Emma, then, is a complex study of self-importance and egotism and malice, as these are absorbed from a society whose morality and values are derived from the economics of class; and a study, further, in the mitigation of these traits, as the heroine comes into partial self-recognition, and at the same time sinks more completely into that society . . . [. . .] This is moral realism . . .

From **Wayne Booth, 'Control of Distance in Jane Austen's *Emma*'**,
in his *Rhetoric of Fiction* (Chicago, Ill. University of Chicago Press, 1961),
pp. 243–66

Wayne Booth represents the 'Chicago School' methodology, which is essentially
formalist literary criticism combined with an interest in the general history of
criticism and literary genres. His influential essay focuses upon narrative voice
and point of view. He argues that the problem for Austen was maintaining the
reader's sympathy for the heroine despite her faults. The reader does not
simply rely upon Mr Knightley's overt criticism of Emma. She makes her the
primary centre of consciousness through which the experience of the novel is
mediated, balancing sympathetic identification of the heroine with detached
criticism. This is achieved through 'free indirect speech', the narrative method
which allowed her to be simultaneously inside and outside her character.

Though Emma's faults are comic, they constantly threaten to produce serious
harm. Yet she must remain sympathetic or the reader will not wish for and delight
sufficiently in her reform.

Obviously, the problem with a plot like this is to find some way to allow the
reader to laugh at the mistakes committed by the heroine and at her punishment,
without reducing the desire to see her reform and thus earn happiness. [. . .]

Sympathy through control of inside views

The solution to the problem of maintaining sympathy despite almost crippling
faults was primarily to use the heroine herself as a kind of narrator, though in third
person, reporting on her own experience. . . . By showing most of the story through
Emma's eyes, the author insures that we shall travel with Emma rather than stand
against her. It is not simply that Emma provides, in the unimpeachable evidence of
her own conscience, proof that she has many redeeming qualities that do not
appear on the surface; such evidence could be given with authorial commentary,
though perhaps not with such force and conviction. Much more important, the
sustained inside view leads the reader to hope for good fortune for the character
with whom he travels, quite independently of the qualities revealed. [. . .]

[. . .] On the one hand she cares about maintaining some sense of mystery as
long as she can. On the other, she works at all points to heighten the reader's sense
of dramatic irony, usually in the form of a contrast between what Emma knows
and what the reader knows.

As in most novels, whatever steps are taken to mystify inevitably decrease the
dramatic irony, and, whenever dramatic irony is increased by telling the reader
secrets the characters have not yet suspected, mystery is inevitably destroyed. The
longer we are in doubt about Frank Churchill, the weaker our sense of ironic
contrast between Emma's views and the truth. The sooner we see through Frank

Churchill's secret plot, the greater our pleasure in observing Emma's innumerable misreadings of his behavior and the less interest we have in the mere mystery of the situation. And we all find that on second reading we discover new intensities of dramatic irony resulting from the complete loss of mystery; knowing what abysses of error Emma is preparing for herself, even those of us who may on first reading have deciphered nearly all the details of the Churchill mystery find additional ironies.

But it is obvious that these ironies could have been offered even on a first reading, if Jane Austen had been willing to sacrifice her mystery. A single phrase in her own name – 'his secret engagement to Jane Fairfax' – or a short inside view of either of the lovers could have made us aware of every ironic touch.

The author must, then, choose whether to purchase mystery at the expense of irony. [. . .]

The reliable narrator and the norms of *Emma*

If mere intellectual clarity about Emma were the goal in this work, we should be forced to say that the manipulation of inside views and the extensive commentary of the reliable Knightley are more than is necessary. But for maximum intensity of the comedy and romance, even these are not enough. The 'author herself' – not necessarily the real Jane Austen but an implied author, represented in this book by a reliable narrator – heightens the effects by directing our intellectual, moral, and emotional progress. . . . But her most important role is to reinforce both aspects of the double vision that operates throughout the book: our inside view of Emma's worth and our objective view of her great faults. [. . .]

[. . .] 'The real evils of Emma's situation were the power of having rather too much her own way, and a disposition to think a little too well of herself; these were the disadvantages which threatened alloy to her many enjoyments. The danger, however, was at present so unperceived, that they did not by any means rank as misfortunes with her.'

None of this could have been said by Emma, and if shown through her consciousness, it could not be accepted, as it must be, without question. Like most of the first three chapters, it is nondramatic summary, building up, through the ostensible business of getting the characters introduced, to Emma's initial blunder with Harriet and Mr Elton. Throughout these chapters we learn much of what we must know from the narrator, but she turns over more and more of the job of summary to Emma as she feels more and more sure of our seeing precisely to what degree Emma is to be trusted. [. . .]

But there are times when Emma and her author are far apart, and the author's direct guidance aids the reader in his own break with Emma. The beautiful irony of the first description of Harriet, given through Emma's eyes (ch. 3) could no doubt be grasped intellectually by many readers without all of the preliminary commentary. But even for the most perceptive its effect is heightened, surely, by the sense of standing with the author and observing with her precisely how Emma's judgment is going astray.

From **Alistair M. Duckworth, '*Emma* and the Dangers of Individualism'**, in his *The Improvement of the Estate: A Study of Jane Austen's Novels* (1971), reprinted with a new preface (Baltimore, Ohio: Johns Hopkins University Press, 1994), pp. 145–79

> Duckworth's influential book sets Austen in her historical context. In his chapter '*Emma* and the Dangers of Individualism', he aligns Emma with that other dangerous innovator Frank Churchill. Duckworth employs binary oppositions to define Austen's social values: conservative stability (represented by Mr Knightley) is contrasted with radical innovation (represented by Frank Churchill). The 'open syntax of manners and morals' is set against the 'concealment and opacity' of games.

With Churchill's entrance, Emma is no longer the puppet-mistress of Highbury but instead becomes a marionette in Churchill's more subtle show.

A dramaturgical vocabulary is inevitable with Churchill, for if he reminds us of any other character in Jane Austen's fiction it is the histrionic Henry Crawford. Like that actor, Churchill is an impresario of some ability. When, on his initial walk through the town, he sights the Crown Inn, 'its character as a ballroom caught him; and instead of passing on, he stopt for several minutes . . . to look in and contemplate its capabilities'. The last word, of course, alerts us to Churchill's desire to 'improve'. Like Crawford at Mansfield or Sotherton, Churchill wishes to introduce movement and flexibility into a landscape of peace and stability. [. . .]

Churchill's pre-eminence in the preparations for the ball – his revised plan for holding it at the Crown – reveal how far he has already usurped Emma's powers of directing and organising. But Churchill's real power over Emma, and the nature of his threat in the novel, are more evident in his love of games. Games are not, of course, introduced by Churchill – the amusing episode of the misunderstood charade announces the motif in the first volume (ch. ix); but it is Churchill who initiates the word game at Hartfield (III, v) and the games on Box Hill (III, vii). Moreover, it is Churchill who makes a running game out of his conversations with Emma on the subject of the mysterious piano – at Mrs Cole's (II, viii), for example, and in Miss Bates's parlour (II, x). [. . .]

Taken cumulatively, however, games carry crucial meaning in *Emma*; they are Jane Austen's means of conveying her apprehension over the continuity of a public and 'open' syntax of morals and of manners. [. . .]

Even before Churchill's entry upon the Highbury scene, the episode of the charade, in exemplifying the concealment and opacity of a game world, had foreshadowed Churchill's behaviour. With his entry a whole vocabulary of concealment begins: nouns like riddle, enigma, conundrum, mystery, equivocation, puzzle, espionage, double-dealing; verbs such as guess, conceal, blind; adjectives such as hypocritical, insidious, suspicious. There is 'doubt in the case' even of his arrival, and Churchill takes care to maintain a doubt as to his motivations and character, not merely because he is secretly engaged to Jane (a transgression of some magnitude in contemporary terms), but also in order to retain his sense of superior manipulation and secret power. His unpredictability is particularly disliked by Mr Knightley, who considers surprises to be 'foolish things'. [. . .]

[. . .] Knightley introduces into *Emma* the serious tone and social commitment that are characteristic of *Mansfield Park*. His call for duty, for the observance of certain prior moral and social imperatives, for consistent and predictable action – these mark Knightley as an exemplary gentleman. [. . .]

Churchill's game-playing is not to be dismissed as venial. It is symptomatic of a world in which once given certitudes of conduct are giving way to shifting standards and subjective orderings. Churchill rejects an inherited body of morals and manners for a little world he himself creates. He is at home in a world of opacity and of separation, preferring it, indeed, to the older world where communication existed by way of public assumptions, for that world required responsibility and consistency, qualities conspicuous by their absence in his character.

From **Marilyn Butler,'*Emma*',** in her *Jane Austen and the War of Ideas* (Oxford: Clarendon Press, 1975), pp. 250–74

> Marilyn Butler presents Austen as an anti-Jacobin novelist,[1] a propagandist of conservative ideology. Butler's study showed how the highly politicized decade of the 1790s saw a flood of novels (often by women) that were engaged in the post-revolutionary 'war of ideas'. Butler sets Austen's novels firmly in the camp of the anti-feminist, traditionalist 'domestic' novels of Mary Brunton and Jane West as opposed to those associated with reformist writers such as Mary Hays and Mary Wollstonecraft. According to this argument, in *Emma* Austen shows her preference for rationality and inherited moral systems over imagination and individual choice. Emma is brought to a recognition of her social duty.

The plot to which the language harmoniously relates is the classic plot of the conservative novel. Essentially, a young protagonist is poised at the outset of life, with two missions to perform: to survey society, distinguishing the true values from the false; and, in the light of this new knowledge of 'reality', to school what is selfish, immature, or fallible in herself. Where a heroine is concerned rather than a hero, the social range is inevitably narrower, though often the personal moral lessons appear compensatingly more acute. Nevertheless the heroine's

---

1 'Jacobin' was the slang name for a political reformer, in allusion to the radical faction (led by Robespierre) that spearheaded the French revolutionary Terror in Paris. The *Anti-Jacobin* (1797–8) was a Tory journal, which satirized radical views. The politically conservative 'domestic' novels of the 1790s were called 'anti-Jacobin'.

classic task, of choosing a husband, takes her out of any unduly narrow or solip-sistic concern with her own happiness. What she is about includes a criticism of what values her class is to live by, the men as well as the women.

The novel with a fallible heroine by its nature places more emphasis on the action than the novel with an exemplary heroine. But *Emma* is an exceptionally active novel. The point is established first of all in the character of the heroine: Emma is healthy, vigorous, almost aggressive. She is the real ruler of the household at Hartfield – in her domestic ascendancy she is unique among Jane Austen's heroines. She is also the only one who is the natural feminine leader of her whole community. Every other Austen leading lady is socially neglected or discounted. It is a misreading of Emma's character to say that she grasps at power, for she neglects rather than exploits her opportunities at Highbury. Jane Austen's purpose in giving her an exceptionally unfettered social position is rather to leave her free to act out her wilful errors, for which she must take entire moral responsibility. [. . .]

Very gradually she is led to the moral trap she falls into on Box Hill [. . .] Box Hill has also been Frank's moral nadir [. . .] it emerges however that by flirting with Emma he has been inflicting intolerable pain upon Jane Fairfax whom he really loves. She is less guilty than Frank in relation to Jane, because, though she sees afterwards that she must have 'stabbed Jane Fairfax's peace in a thousand instances', at the time she is not aware of it. Yet Emma *does* believe Harriet to be in love with the man she is flirting with, and Harriet, no less than Jane, is one of the affronted bystanders. The hurt to Miss Bates is not therefore a single instance, for there is a pattern in the novel of vulnerable single women, whom it is the social duty of the strong and the rich to protect. There is accordingly a continuous link between Emma's errors and Frank's because both arise out of related attitudes to the self and to others. [. . .]

All forms of inwardness and secrecy tend to be anti-social. There is a moral obligation to live outside the self, in honest communication with others [. . .] the theme, then, is the struggle towards a fixed and permanent truth external to the individual; and chastening, necessarily, to individual presumption and self-consequence. [. . .]

The final irony is that this most verbal of novels at last pronounces words themselves to be suspect. It has been called the first and one of the greatest of psychological novels. If so, it resembles no other, for its attitude to the workings of Emma's consciousness is steadily critical. Although so much of the action takes place in the inner life, the theme of the novel is scepticism about the qualities that make it up – intuition, imagination, original insight. Emma matures by submit-ting her imaginings to common sense, and to the evidence. Her intelligence is certainly not seen as a fault, but her failure to question it is. . . . Easily the most brilliant novel of the period, and one of the most brilliant of all English novels, it masters the subjective insights which help to make the nineteenth-century novel what it is, and denies them validity.

From **Julia Prewitt Brown, 'Civilization and the Contentment of Emma'**, in her *Jane Austen's Novels: Social Change and Literary Form* (Cambridge, Mass.: Harvard University Press, 1979), pp. 88–107

Julia Prewitt Brown presents a compelling view of Highbury: far from being static and hierarchical, it more closely resembles a road-map of people, 'a system of interdependence, a community of people all talking to one another, affecting and changing one another: a collection of relationships'. Brown takes issue with the Marxist critic Arnold Kettle (see, **pp. 56–7**). For Brown, the novel is seen not from the perspective of 'frozen class division but from a perspective of living change'. Miss Bates is singled out as a crucial member of society in that she links together all the disparate ranks. Social co-operations and community are vital for protecting vulnerable single women. To ensure the harmony of the community of Highbury, 'the life of the individual must be co-ordinated internally before it can function externally'.

Just as the structure of *Emma* is not causal, it is also not hierarchical. Were we to draw a picture of the novel, it would not, I believe, bring before the reader the ladder of social and moral being that Graham Hough assigns.[1] It would look more like a road map in which the cities and towns, joined together by countless highways and byroads, stood for people. . . .

As the image of a road map suggests, Highbury is a system of interdependence, a community of people all talking to one another, affecting, and changing one another: a collection of relationships. . . . Emma is seen as daughter, sister, sister-in-law, aunt, companion, intimate friend, new acquaintance, patroness, and bride. And each connection lets us see something new in her. [. . .]

Essays on *Emma* have a tendency to describe Highbury the way an ethnographer writes history, sorting through the picked bones of institutions and beliefs. The inner consistency, the living society, escapes attention. Class divisions and difficulties are stressed, and moral traits are eventually viewed as possessions of a particular class, or class attitude. I do not intend to decry this view, but pursued too far, it reduces the society of Highbury to a sack of struggling types in some manner creating order out of chaos. It is not the Highbury Emma sees standing on the doorsteps of Ford's one morning:

> Mr Perry walking hastily by, Mr William Cox letting himself in at the office door, Mr Cole's carriage horses returning from exercise, or a stray letter-boy on an obstinate mule, were the liveliest objects she could presume to expect; and when her eyes fell only on the butcher with his tray, a tidy old woman travelling homewards from shop with her full basket,

---

1   Hough was a Cambridge critic of the Leavisite school, who offered an orthodox 'new critical' reading of the novel in terms of Emma's moral education.

two curs quarrelling over a dirty bone, and a string of dawdling children round the bakers little bow-window eyeing the gingerbread, she knew she had no reason to complain, and was amused enough; quite enough still to stand at the door.

Highbury, it is true, is made up of classes and their individual members. Yet however different the traits of personality and class, they are taken into a functioning society and reshaped by inner organizing forces. Miss Bates is perhaps the nearest symbol of Highbury; all classes join and cooperate in her, just as all gossip passes through her vacant mind. She is the repository of all that occurs and has occurred in Highbury. Her small apartment joins the older gentry (the Woodhouses and Knightleys), the new rich (the Coles), and the lower-middle to lower-class townspeople and clerks. She represents Highbury's fluidity and mobility, its tolerance of past and future classes, or part of the sensibility that helped England avoid a French Revolution. [. . .]

Arnold Kettle points out that it is not necessary for a novelist writing in Jane Austen's time to suggest a solution to the problem of class division and prejudice, but that it is morally necessary for the author to notice the existence of the problem. Jane Austen, he decides, fails to do so. . . . The moral judgement made against *Emma* is disturbingly simple. First of all there are no 'aristocrats' in the novel; even the Churchills are just inflated gentry. Nor does Jane Austen view the landed class as parasitic; she sees it as a functioning part of a changing organism. Mr Knightley manages his land, has little cash, and has a younger brother who makes a living as a lawyer. . . the social world of the novel is peopled with upwardly and downwardly mobile individuals. It is viewed not from the perspective of living change. It is not France in the 1780s, but England at the beginning of the nineteenth century.

The scene at Box Hill possesses great emotional intensity . . . Emma's cruelty completely shocks us. There is something particularly moving and frightening about the rejection of the comic figure in art, such as the rejection of Falstaff (2 *Henry IV*, V.iii) or of the clown in a Charlie Chaplin film . . . Emma's action violates the most basic human law in found in any society whether barbarous or advanced: the protection of the weak . . . Emma delivers the insult because she 'could not resist' . . . there is no reason for it; it is simply a case of unrestrained human hostility. . . . Austen knew that a community like Highbury could be maintained only if its members took a constant, unflagging interest in one another's welfare.

Emma is based on a recognition of the life of the individual as a functioning whole that must be coordinated internally, before it can function externally. [. . .]

This is all the more reason why in *Emma* Jane Austen insists on the necessity and finally the benevolence of social cooperation: because it alone protects the Harriets and the Miss Bateses of the world, cares for, tolerates, and loves them. [. . .]

Emma is a novel of human interdependence in every sense.

From **Sandra M. Gilbert and Susan Gubar, 'Jane Austen's Cover Story (and its Secret Agents)'**, in *The Madwoman in the Attic: The Woman Writer and the Nineteenth-Century Literary Imagination* (1979; reprinted New Haven, Conn.: Yale University Press, 2000), pp. 154–62

> Gilbert and Gubar sketch an engaging picture of a wild and rebellious Jane Austen who unleashed her imagination in the juvenilia, but who learnt to curb and camouflage her rage in her mature work. Under the surface of the submissive 'angel in the house' who accepts patriarchy is the 'madwoman' who erupts in the characters of Mrs Norris, Lady Catherine and Lady Susan. However, in *Emma*, the assertive and rebellious heroine is ultimately punished by being married off to Mr Knightley, who 'will confine her to a life of service and silence'.

Austen's propriety is most apparent in the overt lesson she sets out to teach in all of her mature novels. Aware that male superiority is far more than a fiction, she always defers to the economic, social, and political power of men as she dramatizes how and why female survival depends on gaining male approval and protection. All the heroines who reject inadequate fathers are engaged in a search for better, more sensitive men who are, nevertheless, still the representatives of authority. [. . .]

Dramatizing the necessity of female submission for female survival, Austen's story is especially flattering to male readers because it describes the taming not just of any woman but specifically of a rebellious, imaginative girl who is amorously mastered by a sensible man. No less than the blotter literally held over the manuscript on her writing desk, Austen's cover story of the necessity for silence and submission reinforces women's subordinate position in patriarchal culture. [. . .]

[. . .] A player of word games, a painter of portraits and a spinner of tales, Emma is clearly an avatar of Austen the artist. And more than all the other playful, lively girls, Emma reminds us that the witty woman is responding to her own confining situation with words that become her weapon, a defense against banality, a way of at least *seeming* to control her life. Like Austen, Emma has at her disposal worn-out, hackneyed stories of romance that she is smart enough to resist in her own life. If Emma is an artist who manipulates people as if they were characters in her own stories, Austen emphasizes not only the immorality of this activity, but its cause or motivation: except for placating her father, Emma has nothing to do. Given her intelligence and imagination, her impatient attempts to transform a mundane reality are completely understandable. [. . .]

Yet Austen could not punish her more thoroughly than she does, and in this respect too Emma resembles the other imaginative girls. For all these heroines are mortified, humiliated, even bullied into sense. Austen's heavy attack on Emma, for instance, depends on the abject failure of the girl's wit. The very brilliant and assertive playfulness that initially marks her as a heroine is finally criticized on the grounds that it is self-deluding. Unable to imagine her visions into reality, she finds that she has all along been manipulated as a character in someone else's fiction. Through Emma, Austen is confronting the inadequacy of fiction and the pain of the 'imaginist' who encounters the relentless recalcitrance of the world in which she lives, but she is also exposing the vulnerable delusions that Emma shares with Catherine Morland[1] before the latter learns that she has no story to tell. Not only does the female artist fail, then, her efforts are condemned as tyrannical and coercive. Emma feels great self-loathing when she discovers how blind she has been: she is 'ashamed of every sensation but the one revealed to her – her affection for Mr Knightley – Every other part of her mind was disgusting' (vol. III, ch. 2).

Although Emma is the center of Austen's fiction, what she has to learn is her commonality with Jane Fairfax, her vulnerability as a female. Like the antithetical sisters we have discussed, Jane Fairfax and Emma are doubles. Since they are the most accomplished girls in Highbury, exactly the same age, suitable companions, the fact that they are not friends is in itself quite significant. Emma even believes at times that her dislike for Jane is caused by her seeing in Jane 'the really accomplished young woman which she wanted to be thought herself' (vol. II, ch. 2). In fact, she has to succumb to Jane's fate, to *become* her double through the realization that she too has been manipulated as a pawn in Frank Churchill's game. The seriousness of Emma's assertive playfulness is made clear when she behaves rudely, making uncivil remarks at Box Hill, when she talks indiscreetly, unwittingly encouraging the advances of Mr Elton, and when she allows her imagination to indulge in rather lewd suppositions about the possible sexual intrigues of Jane Fairfax and a married man. In other words, Emma's imagination has led her to the sin of being unladylike, and her complete mortification is a prelude to submission as she becomes a friend of Jane Fairfax, at one with her too in her realization of her own powerlessness. In this respect, Mr Elton's recitation of a well-known riddle seems ominous:

> My first doth affliction denote,
> Which my second is destin'd to feel
> And my whole is the best antidote
> That affliction to soften and heal. –
> (vol. I, ch. 9)

For if the answer is woe/man, then in the process of growing up female Emma must be initiated into a secondary role of service and silence.

---

1 The heroine of *Northanger Abbey*.

From **Jane Nardin, 'Jane Austen and the Problem of Leisure'**, in
D. Monaghan, ed., *Jane Austen in a Social Context* (London: Macmillan, 1981),
pp. 105–22

Jane Nardin examines the plight of the genteel, well-educated and accomplished heroine, whose major problem is that she has too much time on her hands. Emma interferes in the lives of others because she is bored, and has no outlet for her imagination. In contrast to Mr Knightley, who involves himself with those around him, Emma leads a life of isolation and even idleness. Marriage is Emma's salvation because 'as Knightley's wife, she will enter his life of activity and involvement'.

Emma Woodhouse sees herself as the typical eighteenth-century heroine who uses her leisure to become an admirable, accomplished, exemplary woman, and who never suffers a moment's ennui for lack of something to do. She plays, she sings, she draws in a variety of styles, she is vain of her literary attainments and general information, she does the honours of her father's house with style, and confers charitable favours on a variety of recipients – in her own eyes, in fact, she is a veritable Clarissa.[1] But Emma's claims to Clarissahood are hollow. Blessed – or cursed – with money, status, a foolish father and a pliant, though intelligent, governess, Emma has earned admiration too easily. She has not had to apply herself to earn the praise her vanity demands and in fact she has not applied herself. Her music is 'just good enough to be praised' for she is too lazy to practise. Her drawings have 'merit', but it is undeveloped. She makes lists of improving books to read and then does not read them. Her charity is infrequent and yet ostentatious. Further, though she sees herself as a self-reliant woman of resources, who does not need a husband or children to add interest to her life, her undisciplined imagination and her interference with other people's affairs suggest that really she is bored and needs both excitement and a sense that she is accomplishing something. So Emma, who thinks her life demonstrates her ability to use leisure for self-cultivation and the sort of social benefit that comes when a cultured woman uses her good sense to influence others, in fact demonstrates the inability of a talented individual to make herself work when there is no real encouragement to do so. [. . .]

Emma has no work to bring her into contact with others or to occupy her mind and her high status forces her to live in something of a social vacuum. Her very small circle is composed mostly of social inferiors to whom Emma's word is law. Her idleness and laziness stimulate her imagination – for imagination is one way to produce variety and a sense of achievement without actually taking the trouble to do anything. And since Emma is alone a lot and gets little

---

1   Allusion to Samuel Richardson's massive – and massively influential (not least on Austen herself) – epistolary novel of 1747–8, in which the utterly virtuous Clarissa Harlowe is raped by the dashing but evil Lovelace and responds by effectively starving herself to death.

valuable criticism from her cowed acquaintances – Mr Knightley is the only real exception here – she has difficulty realising how often she is mistaken in her opinions. [. . .]

[. . .] Constant activity has made Knightley hardy, constant involvement with others has taught him the pleasure of altruism. Where the humanity of Mr Woodhouse and Emma, rich, idle and uninvolved, shows signs of atrophying from disuse, Knightley's human potential has clearly been developed by his vocational involvements. Where they live locked in worlds created by imagination, he is well-informed and pre-eminently sane. The reader's most convincing guarantee that Emma, at the end of the novel, will become a better woman, derives not from her disillusionments and consequent resolutions – for we have seen her, like characters in *The Idler*, make good resolutions before – but rather from the fact that, as Knightley's wife, she will enter his life of activity and involvement. It is these, and not the individual's resolutions, that are guarantees of sanity and even happiness in the world of *Emma*.

From **David Aers, 'Community and Morality: Towards Reading Jane Austen'**, in D. Aers, J. Cook and D. Punter, *Romanticism and Ideology: Studies in English Writing 1765–1830* (London: Routledge & Kegan Paul, 1981), pp. 118–36

> A harsh view of Austen's politics emerges from David Aers, who applies a Marxist analysis to *Emma*. Austen's idealization of the agrarian, capitalist Mr Knightley and her dismissive treatment of the disenfranchised, such as 'the poor', the gypsies, and even Jane Fairfax, typify her bourgeois ideology. Emma's visit to 'the poor' in particular is viewed as an indication of Austen's own capitalist values, though it should be remembered that Emma's views are not necessarily Jane Austen's, especially as her irony is so often directed against her heroine.

Yet while Mr Knightley is certainly Jane Austen's standard of male excellence (without being infallible), she does present him as an agrarian capitalist, not as some kind of pseudo-feudal magnate. He is prospering well, like his capitalist tenant, Robert Martin, and yet despite his relatively modest lifestyle we are told that he has 'little spare money'. This is because he re-invests his profits, accumulating in good capitalist fashion. Miss Bates notes that Knightley's bailiff-manager 'thinks more about his master's profits than anything', and Knightley himself confesses, 'I would rather be at home looking over William Larkin's week's account' than out dancing. He shows his respect for Martin, whose values he shares, attacks Emma's misconception of Martin's position in the class structure and calls this tenant his 'friend'.

Alongside this, however, Mr Knightley also deploys the Burkian ideology of an organic but fixed, stable, stratified and coherent social order. For example, he comments about Harriet, to Emma:

> Till you chose to turn her into a friend, her mind had no distaste for her own set, nor any ambition beyond it … *she* cannot gain by the acquaintance. Hartfield will only put her out of conceit with all the other places she belongs to. She will grow just refined enough to be uncomfortable with those among whom birth and circumstances have placed her home.

With this Jane Austen tends to agree: '[Harriet] was less and less at Hartfield; which was not to be regretted'. She emphatically accepts the imperatives of social stratification in determining the possibilities of human relationships and simultaneously supports Mr Knightley's anachronistic view of society as a static neo-feudal order where identity is a function of fixed social occupation and place.

[. . .] Furthermore, as we have seen, both Mr Knightley and his tenant are as firmly grounded in the world of late eighteenth-century agrarian capitalism as their author. Mr Knightley in fact manifests practices and perceptions which reflect contradictions in his creator's consciousness and the Tory ideology she represents. [. . .]

[. . .] You can walk around 'large and populous' Highbury, or walk around Mr Knightley's estate and never see a labourer. The system of production is so natural, we are persuaded that it needs no workers. But this nature is the human world of early nineteenth-century agrarian capitalism, involving a specific social and cultural organization to which Mr Knightley's class is committed and one which depends on a specific form of exploiting other people's labour. And ideology which only deals with a central phenomenon (the working classes) by pretending it does not exist is exceptionally vulnerable. Jane Austen senses this fact, and on two separate occasions in *Emma* she gives us her mediation of the agricultural proletariat, the labour side of agrarian capitalism. . . .

The first of these scenes is Emma's visit to 'the poor' . . . [Austen's] own normative values are expressed in this passage:

> Emma was very compassionate; and the distresses of the poor were as sure of relief from her personal attention and kindness, her counsel and patience, as from her purse. She understood their ways, could allow for their ignorance and their temptations, had no romantic expectations of extraordinary virtue from those, for whom education had done so little; entered into their troubles with ready sympathy, and always gave her assistance with as much attention as good will.

This assures the reader that the well-to-do lady is capable of providing material relief for 'the poor'. But certain evasions become apparent, despite the novelist's magisterial tone. By selecting the generalized noun, 'the poor', does Jane Austen mean all 'poor' in the village, that 'large and populous village almost amounting to a town'? No answer emerges. One can also see that the criteria used in deciding who qualifies as 'the poor' Emma should visit and who should be given 'relief' are also not even mentioned. Will the 'relief' still leave them poor and if so exactly what kind of 'relief' is it? [. . .]

I must now pass on to a place where Jane Austen mediates her class's fear of the lower orders loosened from particular ties to land and its gentry. Harriet and her friend are walking along the Richmond road the morning after the ball when they suddenly come across 'a party of gipsies', a group who provide a perfect symbol for the masses of uprooted people who were dispossessed, landless, without regular employment and economic resources. [. . .]

Gipsies, of course, are not literally the labourers who work the land around Highbury, not those who are organized by local overseers of the poor. They represent those who are escaping from 'the iron discipline of the factory' and of the workhouse, and Austen tempts the reader to treat them simply as classless vagrants. They seem a negligible minority barely ruffling the novelist's social ideas and ideology about a coherent society with ranks 'subscribing by assent'. But whereas the visit to 'a poor sick family' mediated her vision of poverty in her society, presenting 'the poor' merely as tame objects for gentry patronage and 'counsel', this scene mediates the worry that below the surface order all is not under control, a fear about the threatening aspect of 'the poor'. To Harriet and her friend, however, they are purely the source of a hysteria which breaks out before any physical challenge whatsoever is offered. This suggests how the hysteria is grounded in the ladies' unarticulated consciousness of a social world composed of dangerous antagonistic groups, their fear and hatred for those not duly respectful of gentry rule and not holding a fixed place in the local community. [. . .]

[. . .] The intelligent, sensitive, educated Jane Fairfax has no capital and no property. She is thus forced to sell her powers on to a 'free' market which will in fact control and deform them. She envisages herself as a commodity she would be 'glad to dispose of', and the analogy of the slave market is a vivid one to reflect the realities of the contemporary situation endured by so many governesses. [. . .]

Many critics continue to venerate Jane Austen as a great artist who is also and inseparably a great 'moralist', while doggedly refusing to discuss the way her work mediates contemporary ideological, moral and social conflicts, unwilling or unable to discuss the way it is informed by a peculiarly Tory ideology and its incoherence. The consequence of this ideology is that instead of her art opening out gentry/middle-class reality and assumptions to a genuinely exploratory fiction which takes alternative forms of life and aspiration seriously, Jane Austen systematically closes up her imagination against critical alternatives. In doing so, her art, her religion, her morality and her version of the individual and community quite fail to transcend the narrow limitations of her historical class, albeit a class whose dominant role in English society is still very evident.

From **Joseph Litvak, 'Reading Characters: Self, Society, and Text in
Emma'** (1985); reprinted in D. Monaghan, ed., _'Emma': Jane Austen_
(New York: St Martin's Press, 1992), pp. 89–109

> Joseph Litvak explores the relationship between games and reading in his
> Derridean[1] analysis of _Emma_ in which he employs a network of puns to demon-
> strate the instability of language, such as 'vehicle', 'ciphers', 'figure'. The novel
> 'stages a battle between figurative language and figuring out, between ciphers
> and deciphering, between Emma's deep superficiality and Knightley's superficial
> depth'.

We might try, then, to read the novel as a contest between Emma and Knightley, a
contest between two equally compelling interpretations of the self – especially the
female self – and society. [. . .]

For though Emma's curriculum may not involve much reading, she and Harriet
spend a great deal of time writing – specifically, 'collecting and transcribing all
the riddles of every sort that [Harriet] could meet with, into a thin quarto of
hot-pressed paper,[2] made up by her friend, and ornamented with cyphers and
trophies'. Here, of course, Knightley could find all the evidence he needs to con-
vict Emma of pedagogical malpractice: not only does the copying of riddles seem
like a stultifying waste of time; the very cover of the riddle book emblematises the
meaninglessness of mere decoration. But, as we have suggested, while 'cyphers'
may escape the stratagems of meaning, they are hardly without significance. We
might remember Austen's 'merely' ornamental analogy for her own art – a 'little
bit (two Inches wide) of Ivory'. Interestingly enough, the 'cyphers' on Harriet's
riddle book exist alongside 'trophies', pictures of prizes. Trophies imply victory –
which in turn implies conflict – and relate etymologically to tropes. As we will see,
this chapter stages a battle between figurative language and figuring out, between
ciphers and deciphering, between Emma's deep superficiality and Knightley's
superficial depth.

'Depth', here, signifies subversive complexity, not just 'strength of mind',
which, as Knightley intimates, presupposes the ability to 'submit' and 'subject'
oneself. Yet if the ciphers on the cover of the riddle book suggest the first kind of
depth, they do so otherwise than by pointing to a plot below – and more politically serious than – what what Gilbert and Gubar call 'Jane Austen's Cover Story'.
For ciphers, as the dictionary reminds us, can be 'texts in secret writing', mono-
grams of some systematically dissimulated referent – in short, riddles. Here one
can judge a book by its cover: the ciphers on the cover of Harriet's book cover the

---

1   That is, influenced by the radically sceptical French philosopher, Jacques Derrida, founder of
     'deconstruction', who argued for the indeterminacy and self-subversion of all meaning and the
     impossibility of any understanding outside the field of 'textuality'.
2   A 'quarto' is defined as a page or paper size resulting from folding a sheet into four leaves, typically
     10 inches × 8 inches. 'Hot pressed' indicates when paper has been smoothed by being pressed
     through hot cylinders.

ciphers inside, which turn out to represent not ultimate truth but merely more covering.

[. . .] How is it, then, that ciphers serve the anti-authoritarian cause? How, in Emma's hands, do they become figures of disruption? How does the play of surfaces in which they are implicated become deep in the subversive sense, rather than in either the authoritarian sense or even the sense that Gilbert and Gubar's notion of a feminist subtext might imply? If the chapter supports authoritarian as well as subversive readings and at the same time dramatises the conflict between them, that conflict is not between figurative language and literal language but between two interpretations of figurative language. Where the 'Knightleian' interpretation grounds figurative language in social rules, the 'Emmaesque' interpretation sees it as inherently ungroundable, even in any politically acceptable subtext.

From **Nancy Armstrong, 'The Self-Contained: *Emma*'**, in her *Desire and Domestic Fiction: A Political History of the Novel* (Oxford, New York: Oxford University Press, 1987), pp. 134–60

In *Desire and Domestic Fiction*, Nancy Armstrong argues that the eighteenth-century domestic novel was an agent of cultural history which created a new form of political power. Taking over from the conduct book, this domestic novel contributed to the empowerment of the middle classes and showed the emergence of a new kind of domestic woman for whom value existed in personal virtue rather than elevated status. Austen's contribution to the rise of the domestic novel resides in the equation she makes between the formation of an ideal community and the formation of a norm of polite English language and character. In *Emma* the emphasis on the need for literacy produces a new and bourgeois form of cultural authority. Though it represents a fictional community, the novel provides a norm of English civility that newly empowered social groups could emulate.

The novel contains other writing than fiction [. . .] It is no wonder, then, that Austen turns away from writing and from the materials of a male education in order to produce the linguistic reforms that will eventually authorise Robert Martin's style of writing. Nor is it any wonder that she turns to gossip and conversation, which are speech modes identified with the female, when she wants to put forth a kind of writing that reveals the true qualities of the individual. [. . .]

By the end of the novel, literacy is no longer represented in such (conduct-book) terms. It is not acquired from writing at all but through mastery of the rules for polite speech. In renouncing the figures of fiction that invariably generate desire where none should be, Emma's speech acquires a kind of politeness that represents emotional truth more accurately than writing presumably ever could. The model for this kind of speech is none other than that which unfolds with the novel's first asseveration: 'Emma Woodhouse, handsome, clever, and rich, with a

comfortable house and happy disposition, seemed to unite some of the best blessings of existence; and had lived nearly twenty-one years in the world with very
little to distress or vex her'. Such a statement appears to constitute writing that
derives from speech rather than from writing. The speech is the speech of the
parlour where behaviour is observed and regulated, and the writing derived from
that speech is a form of writing that uses gossip with all the force and precision of
a diagnostic instrument. [. . .]

If the hierarchy among styles of masculine writing creates a gap between writing and speech in this novel, then the hierarchy among styles of feminine speech
effaces these differences between speech and writing. The writing that is closest to
speech places an author low in a hierarchy of writing, but it is precisely the kind of
English modelled on speech that identifies the well-educated woman. We might
say that Austen attaches gender to writing in order to create a disjunction between
writing and speech. Such disjunction always constitutes a serious crisis in the
organisation of her fictive communities. Producing this crisis allows her not only
to valorise a new kind of writing based on polite speech, but also, and more
importantly, it enables her to situate speech logically prior to writing. In this way,
she uses speech to authorise her preferred style of writing on grounds that the
source of speech, unlike that of writing, resides in the individual. And as she
establishes this as the basis for the truth value of writing, Austen also grants
priority to the verbal practices of women, women who may never carry out pro-
grammes of reading literature, but who are nevertheless essential to maintaining
polite relationships within the community. [. . .]

[. . .] Novels do not have to launch elaborate self-defences anymore, for they
have appropriated the strategies of conduct books to such a degree that fiction . . .
instead of conduct books . . . can claim the authority to regulate reading. . . . I am
suggesting that with Austen, if not with Burney before her, the novel supplants the
conduct book as that writing which declares an alternative, female standard of
polite writing. [. . .]

To read *Emma*, we must not only equate language with power. We must also
equate the language of power with prose that imitates the word spoken by an elite
minority of country gentlefolk quite removed from the centres of power.

From **James Thompson, *Between Self and World: The Novels of Jane
Austen*** (University Park, Pa.: Pennsylvania State University Press, 1988),
pp. 159–210

As a Marxist, James Thompson believes that Austen's novels are time-bound
and historical and enact the bourgeois ideology of the period. He analyses the
complexities and contradictions between the language of (public) social obligation and the 'feeling' of (private) individual interiority in *Emma*. The individual's
sense of 'alienation' in capitalist society turns within for 'true authenticity'.
Thompson focuses on Austen's treatment of marriage in *Emma*, as a union
promising 'true intimacy' against the threat of loneliness and solipsism.

In Austen, the extended family is not seen as a haven in a heartless world, but rather as something suffocating, a mediating stage between the larger public world and the private world of intimacy. The place of privacy in Austen and the narrative pattern that is determined by it can be explored through Austen's use of key terms that represent social and personal relations: *intimacy, reserve, openness*, and *solitude*. [. . .]

The process by which false intimacies are exploded and true intimacies are disrupted is most fully worked out in *Emma*, in which Austen appears to be exploring most consciously and carefully the dangers of false intimacy and the value of true intimacy. Here especially, Austen works with a series of contrasts: Emma's former closeness with Mrs Weston is set against her friendship with Harriet Smith; this friendship, or more properly, this patronage of Harriet is set in competition with Mrs Elton's patronage of Jane Fairfax. Through these contrasts, the reader is regularly shown that Emma prefers the insipid company and unequal friendship of Harriet Smith to the more valuable or more equal and thus more challenging friendship expected but spurned between herself and Jane Fairfax. In this particular relationship, the values of intimacy are explicitly contrasted with the repeated accusations of reserve that make Jane so repulsive in Emma's eyes. Overall, the remarkable sense of community that makes this novel so extraordinary at every point suggests both the values of and the constrictions inherent in a tiny community where everyone of the same class is inevitably and necessarily on familiar footings with the others. [. . .]

Nevertheless, although Emma spends most of this novel surrounded and almost strangled by intimate friends and acquaintances, she, like all of the other heroines, finds herself very much alone just before the end of the story. . . . By the end, she is forced to see that it is difficult to know one's own feelings, more difficult to express those feelings to another, and impossible, finally to know the other's sensations.

The twin threats of loneliness and solipsism serve to emphasise the value of true intimacy: if Emma can never know the inside of Jane Fairfax, the novel is constructed so as to lead us up to the expectation that she can, eventually, know Mr Knightley. Closing the pattern of false, failed, and broken intimacies, the final marriage serves to mark the expectation and the hope that true intimacy can exist. Austen nowhere examines happy marriage within her novels proper, but her novels are constructed so as to lead up to the hope that such happiness is possible, lying just on the other side, as it were, of the last page of the novel. In this sense, Austen's are novels of courtship but not of marriage, for they always end on the threshold of marriage, where intimate happiness is indicated in the future tense, as something about to be experienced, but not experienced and verified quite yet. True intimacy does not exist within the novel proper because Austen indicates that it cannot be portrayed. This failure to portray suggests less that she does not finally believe in it or that she herself does not know how to express it than that she believes it is not expressible. . . . In Austen's novels, marital happiness is dependent upon knowledge of the other, and full knowledge of the other is another word for intimacy.

From **Claudia L. Johnson, 'Emma: "Woman, Lovely Woman Reigns Alone"'**, in her *Jane Austen: Women, Politics and the Novel* (Chicago, Ill.: University of Chicago Press, 1988), pp. 121–43

In contrast to Gilbert and Gubar, Claudia Johnson shows how Austen corroborates her faith in the fitness of Emma's rule. By inviting us to consider the contrasts between the rule of Emma and that of Mrs Elton, Austen is able to 'explore positive versions of female power': 'Considering the contrast between Emma and Mrs Elton can enable us to distinguish the use of social position from the abuse of it'. The novel concludes not with an endorsement of patriarchy, but with a marriage between equals. Furthermore, this is shown in the 'extraordinary' ending which sees Knightley giving up his own home to share Emma's and thus giving his 'blessing to her rule'.

In stunning contrast with *Mansfield Park*, where husbands dominate their households with as little judiciousness as decency, in *Emma* woman *does* reign alone. Indeed, with the exception of Knightley, all of the people in control are women: Mrs Churchill's whims as well as her aches and pains are felt, discussed, and respected miles away from her sofa; at least some, if not all, people in the neighborhood accept Mrs Elton's ministrations as 'Lady Patroness'; and Emma's consciousness that she is considered 'first' in consequence at Highbury may peeve her critics, but it does not faze her neighbors, and no one – least of all Mr Knightley – questions her right to preeminence.

In its willingness to explore positive versions of female power, *Emma* itself is an experimental production of authorial independence unlike any of Austen's other novels. [. . .]

[. . .] Mrs Weston does not share Knightley's dire predictions about Emma's projects, because she considers her judgment worth relying on: 'where Emma errs once, she is in the right a hundred times'. Here is no blind dependence on the infallibility of Emma's authority, but instead a confidence in its basic soundness: 'She has qualities which may be trusted; she will never lead any one really wrong; she will make no lasting blunder.'

Emma amply corroborates Mrs Weston's faith in the fitness of Emma's rule, but often so tactfully as to be almost imperceptible. This tact, however, is necessary first of all because Emma's best actions are of the sort which she, unlike Mrs Elton, disdains to trumpet. A few strokes of the pen, for example, show that in her attentions to the poor and afflicted of her parish, Emma is intelligent, generous, compassionate, and – whatever she is in her studies – steady. Further, although Knightley thinks her 'rather negligent' in contributing to the 'stock' of Miss Bates's 'scanty comforts', Emma's 'own heart' ranks visits there an obligation. She is not shown to fuss over sending that hind-quarter of pork to the Bateses – though her father would mull and send less – and when she does explain to Knightley that respect for her father's peace prevents her from making her carriage of use to her neighbors, he smiles with conviction. Because she nowhere styles herself 'Lady Patroness,' we can only assume that Emma considers the performance of untold acts of kindness a duty attached to her social position requiring no announcement or praise.

Considering the contrast between Emma and Mrs Elton can enable us to distinguish the use of social position from the abuse of it, a proper sense of office from a repulsive officiousness; and in the process it offers a glimpse of the conservative model of social control working well. The principle of difference between the two women and their rules is not finally reducible to class. What makes Mrs Elton intolerable is not that she is new money and Emma is old, and that Mrs Elton thus only pretends to prerogatives of status Emma comes by honestly. Mrs Elton's exertions of leadership set our teeth on edge because of their insistent publicity, not because of their intrinsic fraudulence. [. . .]

[. . .] But Emma is an authority figure responsive to the morally corrective influence of public opinion. This is what makes her feel the truth of Knightley's reproach at Box Hill, and this is what makes her resolute, swift, and feeling in her amends. [. . .]

Such is the consummate mastery of Austen's plotting here that Emma's misapprehensions seem utterly plausible when we read the novel for the first time, and she appears wilfully to 'misread' the sunny clarity of truth only when our own repeated readings of this romance, the stuff of literary criticism, have laid her misconstructions bare. [. . .]

But Knightley and Emma stand on an equal footing. [. . .] For Knightley, advice is not a function of power. He does not assume that the parental liberty he takes in reproaching due him – indeed it is a 'privilege rather endured than allowed'. Being who and what she is, Emma dishes out almost as much as she gets, and when she does not follow his advice – which is almost always – he does not turn away.

The conclusion of *Emma* shares the polyvalence characteristic of the endings in Austen's later novels. [. . .] As Emma well knows, Knightley's move into Hartfield is extraordinary considering his own power and independence: 'How very few of those men in a rank of life to address Emma would have renounced their own home for Hartfield!' The conclusion which seemed tamely and placidly conservative thus takes an unexpected turn, as the guarantor of order himself cedes a considerable portion of the power which custom has allowed him to expect. In moving to Hartfield, Knightley is sharing *her* home, and in placing himself within her domain, Knightley gives his blessing to her rule.

From **John Wiltshire, '*Emma*: "the Picture of Health"** ', in his *Jane Austen and the Body* (Cambridge: Cambridge University Press, 1992), pp. 110–54

Jane Austen has been seen as a novelist who avoids the physical. John Wiltshire shows the importance of bodies in her text, and Austen's emphasis on health and illness in *Emma*. Wiltshire draws upon medical and feminist theories of 'the body'.

Through its comfortable concern with its denizens' well-being, the novel poses a series of important questions, I suggest, about the nature of health, which are put more insistently through its gallery of sufferers from so-called 'nervous' disorders. Not only does Isabella Knightley, as might be expected, complain of 'those little nervous head-aches and palpitations which I am never entirely free from any where', but even placid Harriet, even Mrs Weston, let alone Jane Fairfax, suffer from, or complain of these symptoms called 'nerves'. But the two grand embodiments of the nervous constitution in *Emma* are Mr Woodhouse and Mrs Churchill and they preside, one way or another, over the novel's action. [. . .]

[. . .] Mrs Weston does not mean that Emma instantiates some general quality 'Health', but that the quality, 'health', cannot be better known than by Emma's embodiment of it. As far as Mrs Weston is concerned, she *is* health, and health is realized in her beauty. What – in the largest sense – health is, is to be known in the activity of the life that is Emma's, in what I have called her spirit: not a moral quality in itself, and certainly not guaranteeing laudable or ethically admirable conduct, but appealing to an understanding of another's life on a larger ground than that of the moral philosopher and ethicist whom Knightley here represents. [. . .]

Jane Fairfax is the shadowy background, the obscured antithesis to the heroine, and her story contributes much to the chiaroscuro of this picture of health. Jane's health is frail, and her beauty, unlike Emma's, is no assurance of vitality. Her presentation takes up the issues present more sketchily in the references to Mrs Churchill. Although she acts and speaks directly in the text, her position within it, her reserve and her secret forbid access to her inner life. What is therefore understood of her is constructed on the site of her body, her 'look', which depending on the observer, can signify either propensity to ill-health or beauty and distinction. In the absence of open speech, Emma, like her neighbours, is perpetually reading Jane's body. Her prejudice against Jane (and her own abundant health) make her unresponsive to certain aspects of the sensitive and cultivated woman whom she ought to have made her friend, but the proneness to illness, the precariousness of Jane's condition, is discernible, even though, after her introduction by the narrator in the second volume, Jane is perceived – glimpsed would be a better word – largely through Emma's eyes. The narrator introduces Jane as an orphan, whose mother died 'overcome with consumption and grief' and it is the fear of TB, 'the standing apprehension of the family' that apparently motivates her aunt's continual fussing ('Did you remember your tippet?'), Highbury's neighbourly concern over her walks in the rain, as well as Knightley's urgent action to prevent her overtaxing herself by singing. [. . .]

If we were to follow Mr Perry on his rounds in Highbury, then, we would learn a good deal about the social politics of illness, about the power-relations of illness behaviour, and about the attribution of meanings to bodies and faces. But the novel in which he so elusively features goes beyond an anthropology or political analysis of illness, to a larger concern – a metaphysics or epistemology of health. Enclosing her heroine within a community preoccupied with, and talking constantly about, ill health, Jane Austen conducts an investigation, though not of course in abstract terms, into the meaning – moral, spiritual, psychological, physical – of health. Working through and beneath the novel's amused depiction of bodily events as the focus and currency of power-relations is a larger and more urgent enterprise, which is something to do with manifesting, displaying, declaring the condition of good health.

From **Valentine Cunningham, 'Games Texts Play'**, in her *In the Reading Gaol: Postmodernity, Texts, and History* (Oxford: Blackwell, 1994), pp. 259–337

> Valentine Cunningham's reading of *Emma* is another one that uncovers the slippery nature of the novel's language. For Cunningham, Mr Knightley is a fallible figure who fails to uncover the third anagram in the alphabet game. Though family tradition claims that the third anagram is 'pardon', the 'text is silent', thus revealing to the reader 'the enigmatic difficulties of reading'. Cunningham plays with the various meanings and interpretations of the word 'Frank', from 'franking' letters, to Frank's lack of Frankness: 'Clearly the nature of frankness – what it means to be frank and Frank – is under frank inspection'. At the core of *Emma* is 'the so unfrank doings of the unfrank franker of unfrank letters'.

It's part of a sense of knowing where we are in our reading of Emma through the riddling going on through and around her. When we come, though, to Frank Churchill's alphabet game the sense of word-games as no joke continues, but now it's the reader's own hermeneutic[1] footing that becomes unsure. In chapter 41 *Emma* plays riddling games with the reader as well as with the characters. [. . .] The hermeneutical difficulties of reading, of epistles and texts in general, are emblematized in the puzzle of these particular letters of the alphabet and the words Churchill forms from them. He makes two or three alphabetical clusters: *blunder, Dixon*, and possibly also a third word which remains, however, unspecified. What does all this signify? What, especially is that last word? What *is* Churchill's game? [. . .] But even more arresting is the truly stubborn enigma of the third word.

'Mr Knightley thought he saw another collection of letters anxiously pushed towards her, and resolutely swept away by her unexamined.' In the general confusion of guests leaving, he cannot be certain whether any word has actually passed. Nor is he clear about the mood of the suspicious pair: 'how they parted, Mr Knightley could not tell'. That the novel's most acute observer and moral censor is so confused is to be felt by the reader as particularly telling. And the confusion is one endorsed by the text. The Austen family liked to continue the puzzling out of this particular word-game: family tradition had it that this third word was *pardon* – Churchill apologizing for the *Dixon* jest that so hurt Jane's

---

1 'Hermeneutics' is the technical term for the art of interpretation.

feelings. But our text remains silent. In other words, the novel's insistence upon the enigmatic difficulties of reading is absorbingly strengthened at this point. [. . .]

What we are confronted with in *Emma*, what *Emma* confronts, is, in other words, the problematic frankness or candour of letters. Frankness is obviously in question in *Emma*. When a key protagonist in a fictional episode of covert letter-writing, the transgressive circulation of undercover meanings, is named Frank, you should certainly prick up your ears and look for trouble. To be frank is to be open and outspoken; which Frank Churchill is not, at least, not when it comes to his affair with Jane Fairfax. At the time of *Emma*, to frank a letter was to put your signature on its outside and so own up before the world to being its sender; which is not the nature of Frank Churchill's correspondence with Jane. Clearly the nature of frankness – what it means to be frank and Frank – is under frank inspection. What perturbs this novel is precisely the lack of openness in *Emma*'s world, and it's a lack provocatively embodied, it turns out, in the bearer of a name that's utterly central to the vocabulary of sincerity: one Frank. So Jane Austen's usual moral lexicography has focused – unusually for her: no Dickens she – in a proper noun, a personal name. More usually in her fictions the sharp-tongued moral lexicographer sticks to probing the semantics of the common nouns and adjectives of moral praise and blame, the traditional novelist's verbal tools of description and discrimination – good, better, best, kind, wrong, amiable, and the like. When Knightley criticizes Churchill for a lack of English amiability ('He may be very "aimable" . . .' (ch. 18)) he's only doing Jane Austen's customary hatchet-job of moral lexicography. Which is momentous enough. But when this novel, with the so unfrank doings of the unfrank franker of unfrank letters Frank Churchill at its core, focuses its moral-lexical doubting through the then currently uncertain meanings of the words *candid* and *candour*, something rather special, and even rather momentously exemplary, does seem to be going on, even for Jane Austen.

From **Claudia L. Johnson, ' "Not at all what a man should be!":** **Remaking English Manhood in *Emma*'**, in her *Equivocal Beings: Politics, Gender, and Sentimentality in the 1790s* (Chicago, Ill.: University of Chicago Press, 1995), pp. 191–205

Here, Johnson takes issue with the post-war male critics, such as Mudrick, Wilson and Schorer for their fixation on Emma's 'coldness', her lack of hetero-sexual feeling, and even her 'manliness'. She argues that they do not take into account the 'slippages of sex and gender' in relation to the social events of the day. Austen does not apologize for Emma's independent 'masculinity', as the gender transgression that she is most concerned with is on the masculine side. Johnson 'historicizes the treatment of femininity *and* masculinity in *Emma*.' In particular, she draws attention to the construction of masculinity in the novel, as it reflects the changes in society and literature. Mr Woodhouse as the 'man of feeling' of the late eighteenth-century has now become something of 'a joke', as

definitions of masculinity have changed and evolved. Mr Knightley may represent a masculine ideal, yet his masculinity is not traditional but new, 'he does not
make a big deal out of sexual difference'. Rather than being a gallant or sentimental figure, he is 'humane' and 'fraternal'. The novel also ridicules
conventionally feminine characters, such as Isabella Knightley, as well as conventionally masculine figures, such as Frank Churchill. Johnson shows how, for
Austen, masculine self-definitions were not a given, but were 'qualities under
reconstruction'.

A long time before feminists came along, 'classic' Austenian critics considered the
sex and gender transgression of Emma their business. [. . .] Pained as I am by the
cheeriness of their misogyny, I also think they were basically right about Emma:
quite susceptible to the stirrings of homoerotic pleasure, Emma *is* enchanted by
Harriet's soft blue eyes; displaying all the captivating enjoyment of 'a mind
delighted with its own ideas', Emma *is* highly autonomous and autoerotic; and,
finally, displaying shockingly little reverence for dramas of heterosexual love,
Emma's energies and desires are *not* fully contained within the grid imposed by
the courtship plot . . . Austen never faults Emma's 'masculine spirit'. Postwar
critics groove on what they are pleased to call Emma's *humiliation*, her *chastise-
ment*, her *submission*. But *Emma* is not interested in subjecting the masculine
independence of its heroine to disciplinary correctives. [. . .]

Where this novel *is* concerned with gender transgression, it is from the masculine, not the feminine side. What 'true' masculinity is like – what a 'man' is, how a
man speaks and behaves, what a man really wants – is the subject of continual
debate, even when characters appear to be discussing women. [. . .]

[. . .] 'Classic' Austenian critics assumed the constancy of feminine norms, and
policed Emma's womanhood accordingly, but they sometimes cast an eye
towards errant males too . . . Edmund Wilson appears to have been the first to call
Mr Woodhouse a 'silly old woman'. . . . Mudrick once again follows suit when he
declares that Mr Woodhouse possesses no 'masculine trait', that he is 'really an
old woman' [see **p. 55**] [. . .]

The assumption behind these readings is that there is one, continuous mode of
manliness against which Mr Woodhouse is to be judged. [. . .] Historically considered, far from being an unusual, deviant, emasculated, or otherwise deficient
figure, Mr Woodhouse represents the ideal of sentimental masculinity . . . The
qualities that typify him – sensitivity, tenderness, 'benevolent nerves,' allegiance
to the good old ways, courtesies to the fair sex, endearing irrationality, and even
slowness, frailty, and ineptitude itself – also typify the venerated paternal figures
crowding the pages of Burney and Radcliffe, to say nothing of those of Edmund
Burke. [. . .]

Emma is written after the crisis that launched the re-emergence of male senti-
mentality had abated. In it, this tradition of sentimental masculinity is archaic,
and it has become somewhat of a joke. Mr Woodhouse is dearly beloved and
fondly indulged, but his sensitivity is not revered. The novel works instead to

redefine masculinity. We will miss what is distinctive about Austen's achievement if we assume that masculine self-definitions were givens rather than qualities under reconstruction. Critics commonly agree that Mr Knightley represents an ideal, but what has *not* been adequately appreciated, I think, is the novelty of that ideal, for by representing a 'humane' rather than 'gallant' hero, Austen desentimentalizes and deheterosexualizes virtue, and in the process makes it accessible to women as well. [. . .]

[. . .] The real man, it is implied here, is a man of few words. Whereas an earlier generation of sentimental men had made a spectacle of their affect – of honorable feelings so powerful as to exceed all possibility of control, thus saturating handkerchiefs and liberally bedewing eloquent pages – the manful Mr Knightley retreats from display, cultivating containment rather than excess, and 'burying under a calmness that seemed all but indifference' the 'real attachment' he feels towards his brother and towards Emma as well. And this new, plain style of manliness is a matter of national import, constituting the *amiable*, 'the true English style,' as opposed of course, to the *aimable*, the artificial, the courtly, the dissembling, the servile, and (as the tradition goes) the feminized French. [. . .]

Emma puts pressure not on deviance from femininity, then, but on deviance from masculinity. . . . The more conventionally feminine women in the novel – one thinks of Harriet, who is willing to marry any man who asks; of Mrs Elton, with her fulsome little love-names for her husband; or of Isabella, whose wifely devotion verges on sheer stupidity – gives heterosexuality a rather revolting appearance, against which Emma's coolness looks sane and enviable. [. . .]

Emma disdains not only the effeminacy of men, but also the femininity of women . . . conventional femininity is a degradation to which Emma does not submit.

From **Juliet McMaster, 'Class'**, in Edward Copeland and Juliet McMaster, eds, *The Cambridge Companion to Jane Austen* (Cambridge: Cambridge University Press, 1997), pp. 115–30

Juliet McMaster's essay presents a more balanced picture of Austen's class affiliations than that offered in some of the more stridently ideological criticism of the 1980s, setting her in a system that was changing and evolving, and revealing her as one who personally suffered from the inequities of her social system. Characters are seen to be on the way down the social ladder, as well as upwardly mobile. The Bateses are on the way down, as Mr Perry is on the way up, with his intention to buy a carriage. McMaster shows how Mr Knightley does not exploit his rank: for example, he walks to a ball in preference to using his carriage. McMaster's Austen 'doesn't share the snobbish prejudice against trade, she pays close attention to the gradual assimilation of the trading classes into gentility'. In this subtle argument, class is closely aligned to manners, and it is Emma's, not her creator's, snobbish attitudes that have to be corrected.

Class difference was of course a fact of life for Austen, and an acute observation of the fine distinctions between one social level and another was a necessary part of her business as a writer of realistic fiction. Nor would she have wished it away, although at the time of writing her novels, she herself – as the unmarried daughter of a deceased country clergyman, like Miss Bates – knew what it was to suffer from the class system. [. . .]

Mr Knightley (whose knightly moral status is expressed in his name rather than a literal title) . . . walks, when status-conscious people like the Osbornes in *The Watsons* would make a point of riding in a carriage . . . Like an expensive car today, carriages were status symbols . . . Perry postpones the purchase; but we are given reason to believe that in due course he will indeed rise to the carriage-owning class. [. . .]

Austen locates few major characters in 'trade', and for many of her characters the word has a ring that seems to require apology. It is not surprising that the gentry and professional classes felt somewhat threatened by the large changes that were coming with the Industrial Revolution, and tended to close ranks against the newly powerful and the *nouveaux riches*. Trade represents new money, and money, like wine, isn't considered quite respectable until it has aged a little. Austen is clearly fascinated by this process: though she doesn't share the snobbish prejudice against trade, she pays close attention to the gradual assimilation of the trading classes into gentility. Emma Woodhouse again can represent the snobbish position, at least in her initial reaction, on the rise of the Cole family in Highbury. But it is important to notice that Emma's attitude evolves and changes. The Coles, as Emma places them, are 'of low origin, in trade, and only moderately genteel'. [. . .]

Much has to do with manners and tact. However reluctantly, Emma accepts the Coles into the genteel society of Highbury, because they 'expressed themselves so properly', they show 'real attention'. The new Mrs Elton, however, is another matter. Before meeting her Emma has ascertained that she is 'the youngest of the two daughters of a Bristol – merchant, of course, he must be called' (the dread word 'tradesman' may not be uttered). But she conscientiously withholds judgment until she meets the bride in person. When she does appear, Mrs Elton confirms Emma's worst prejudices: Emma can't stand her 'airs of pert pretension and under-bred finery'. Moreover, nor can most readers. It is a difficult exercise in discrimination to pick apart social standing, manners, and morals. But Austen enables us to distinguish between Emma's unapproved social snobbery and her proper moral aversion to Mrs Elton's loud-mouthed self-approval. For instance, like Miss Bingley, Mrs Elton regularly uses her newly acquired status to put down others. [. . .]

If those involved in trade hover on the brink of gentility, there are many grades and degrees below them. Mrs and Miss Bates in *Emma* are similarly poised, and a gulf of poverty yawns below them. They are of a class that was later to be called 'shabby-genteel', people who have come down in the world. Once prominent as the wife of the vicar, Mrs Bates as a widow lives on slender means, in cramped quarters in an upstairs apartment, with only one servant, a maid-of-all-work. But though she and her daughter are short of money and can't entertain, they still have *connections*: they are on visiting terms with the best families of Highbury;

and that's more than can be said, as we have seen, for the Coles, with all their money and servants.

Another kind of amphibian, one who can move upwards or sink downwards in society, is the governess. Jane Fairfax, for instance, is well bred and well educated, beautiful and talented. But because her relatives cannot support her, she must earn her living at one of the only professions available to women, as a governess. . . . Jane Fairfax speaks in poignant terms of employment agencies for governesses: 'offices for the sale – not quite of human flesh – but of human intellect'. The alignment with the slave trade is explicit; there is a passing hint, too, of prostitution. Jane Fairfax, like Jane Eyre, is one of those governesses who survive by marrying into the gentry. But her escape from a life of drudgery, looking after Mrs Smallridge's three children for a pittance, is a narrow one.

From **Edward Copeland, 'Money',** in Edward Copeland and Juliet McMaster, eds, *The Cambridge Companion to Jane Austen* (Cambridge: Cambridge University Press, 1997), pp. 131–48

> Copeland places Austen in a culture based on economics and in particular the acquisition of commodities: she uses consumerism as a way of exploring society.

. . . *money*, especially money as spendable income, is the love-tipped arrow aimed at the hearts of Jane Austen's heroines and her readers: first of all, for its power to acquire the material goods that can support the all-important signs of her rank's claims to genteel station; second, as the prod of anxiety that focuses its own potential for loss. In her novels, Austen approaches the subject, money, from three different, but related, points of view. First, as a member of the pseudo-gentry, that is to say, the upper professional ranks of her rural society; second, as a woman in that society, severely handicapped by law and custom from possessing significant power over money; finally, as a novelist who joins other women novelists in a larger conversation about money. [. . .]

In [*Emma*], Austen chooses consumer signs, those social markers so important to her own class, to explore society. The action in *Emma* rides forward on a great tide of new consumer display. Mr Weston buys a small estate; the former Miss Taylor, now Mrs Weston, gets a new house, a new husband, and a new carriage; Jane Fairfax receives, mysteriously, a Broadwood piano; the Coles have a new dining room and a new pianoforte that none of them can play; Emma has a new round dining table; Frank Churchill buys gloves at Ford's, and Harriet Smith buys ribbons; Mr Elton goes to Bath for a new wife and a new carriage; Mrs Elton boasts lace and pearls and more servants than she can remember; Mrs Perry yearns for a new carriage; and the Martins have 'a very handsome summer-house, large enough to hold a dozen people'. There are also more homely items on offer: plenty of good wine at Mr Weston's; sweetbreads and asparagus at Mr Woodhouse's; a hind quarter of pork for Miss Bates from Hartfield; apples for Miss Bates from Donwell Abbey; arrowroot for Jane Fairfax from Hartfield; and walnuts for Harriet Smith from Mr Martin, who walks 'three miles around' to get them, though he forgets to enquire for the novels she had mentioned. [. . .]

But consumer goods in *Emma* also trace a society in restless motion. The Coles are on the way up with their new dining room, new pianoforte, and an increase in their servants; Mrs and Miss Bates and Jane Fairfax are on their way down with their economies, modest quarters, and one maid. Mr Martin is on the way up, as are the Eltons, the Coxes, the Smallridges, and the Sucklings. People are passing so rapidly through the gradations of income and the consumer markers associated with them that the old rules of birth and social order are thrown into question.

Mr Woodhouse, who likes everything that is old and settled, marks one end of the scale; Mrs Elton, who likes everything that is new and in motion, marks the other. Emma herself is in a state of confusion, blinded by vanity and social snobbery, but also blinded by the very consumer signs that offer themselves so temptingly to her imagination. Her conclusions about Jane Fairfax's pianoforte are her most embarrassingly public mistake, but her persistent inability to judge behaviour in her society turns, like a scorpion, on the novel itself, the consumer object whose self-proclaimed mandate to interpret social signs most consistently misleads her. [. . .]

If Emma had only read past the consumer signs of her society (false and misleading) to see and read the 'real' signs of social behaviour before her eyes (true and abiding) then she would not have made such a distressing hash of the situation. But here consumer fiction proves double false. . . . Austen's society is experiencing major social change, fuelled in some degree by the very goods – novels among the first – that set themselves up as signs of social truths. The most unexpected people are indeed climbing the social ladder with the aid of money and the social markers it buys.

From **Jonathan Bate, 'Culture and Environment: from Austen to Hardy'**, *New Literary History*, no. 30 (1999). Reprinted in Jonathan Bate, *The Song of the Earth* (London: Picador and Cambridge, Mass.: Harvard University Press, 2000), pp. 5–6

As part of an ecological analysis of Romantic period literature, Jonathan Bate shows how the very essence of what Austen regards as authentic national identity, 'English verdure, English culture, English comfort', is derived 'not from a set of political institutions based in London' – monarchy, parliament and so forth – but from 'the harmonious play, suggested by the verbal euphony', of 'verdure' and 'culture' (meaning agriculture).

Here is Emma Woodhouse, surveying the view from the grounds of Donwell Abbey, the home of George Knightley:

> The considerable slope, at nearly the foot of which the Abbey stood, gradually acquired a steeper form beyond its grounds; and at half a mile

distant was a bank of considerable abruptness and grandeur, well clothed with wood; – and at the bottom of this bank, favourably placed and sheltered, rose the Abbey-Mill Farm, with meadows in front, and the river making a close and handsome curve around it.

It was a sweet view – sweet to the eye and the mind. English verdure, English culture, English comfort, seen under a sun bright, without being oppressive.

The knightly Mr Knightley takes his Christian name, George, from England's patron saint. He embodies a value-structure which remains profoundly Christian, but which has shifted from pious observance to secular virtue. His house is on the site of a former abbey. A place that was once consecrated to the spiritual good life, to the vertical relationship between humankind and God, it is now consecrated to the social good life: it has become an emblem of productive and harmonious rural being. Instead of being drawn upward to the heavens, the eye looks out horizontally to the well-ordered environment.

The abbey occupies a safe middle ground, below a hill and above a river. It is surrounded by mature woodland that signifies Knightley's willingness to take the long view of profit – potential timber is an investment for future generations. The farm is below the abbey in the landscape, as the gentleman farmer Robert Martin is below Mr Knightley in the social order, but it is protected by its environment, as the interests of Martin are cared for by Knightley. The weather – 'a sun bright, without being oppressive' – is made one with the social structure. Here Austen is inheritor of a long tradition of European thought which associated a temperate climate with a liberal society and excessive heat with oriental despotism.

'English verdure, English culture, English comfort' are thus embedded in a particular landscape. What Austen regards as authentic national identity is derived not from a set of political institutions based in London – monarchy, parliament and so forth – but from the harmonious play, suggested by the verbal euphony, of 'verdure' and 'culture'. 'Verdure' is natural greenness, the product of England's wet weather, while 'culture' is intended to imply the mixed farmland of traditional English farming methods.

From **Brian Southam, 'Emma: England, Peace and Patriotism'**, in his *Jane Austen and the Navy* (London: Hambledon and London, 2000), pp. 239–56

B. C. Southam views Mr Knightley as a traditional 'John Bull' figure, the embodiment of Cobbett's[1] 'resident *native* gentry', a progressive farmer, whose very Englishness typifies Austen's patriotic intent. In contrast to the Marxist critics

---

1   William Cobbett (1763–1835), polemical essayist who was simultaneously a political radical and a conservative apologist for the old-style landowners who cared for their land and their labourers, as opposed to the new *rentier* class of often-absentee rural landlords for whom agriculture was commerce and nothing more.

In *Emma* . . . Patriotism is held up for our inspection and the traditional enmity between England and France is played out in the antipathy between George Knightley, a gentlemanly John Bull, and the Frenchified Frank Churchill . . . Towards the end of *Emma*, when enlightenment dawns, Emma sees the course of deception which Frank Churchill and Jane Fairfax have practised on Highbury as a 'system of secrecy and concealment, a system of hypocrisy and deceit – espionage and treachery' . . . 'espionage', a word recently arrived in English and still regarded as heavily French. [. . .]

The Frenchness of Churchill's unmanly behaviour is also signalled by his 'finessing', a *finesse* (in Johnson's *Dictionary* treated as a French word) being a trick or a stratagem . . . The process of linguistic labelling is carried a stage further when Knightley sizes up Churchill's 'smooth, plausible manners' with definitions which are explicitly nationalistic:

> your amiable young man can be amiable only in French, not in English.
> He may be very 'aimable', have very good manners, and be very agreeable; but he can have no English delicacy towards the feelings of other people: nothing really amiable about him.

The contrast here is between French veneer, the art of pleasing . . . and the solid worth of English 'really amiable' by Knightley's definition – a meaning lost to us today – a quality of thoughtfulness and consideration for others. [. . .]

In identifying the particular quality of Knightley's patriotism, our best guide is Cobbett's *Rural Rides*, a collection of the reports he made in the 1820s from journeys undertaken to enquire into the state of the countryside. He observed the signs of economic and social decline and the plight of the farming communities from county to county. Cobbett associated the rising levels of agricultural poverty and discontent with the arrival over the last twenty or thirty years of a new breed of land-owner, the war-profiteers (as he saw them) who were now displacing the traditional squirearchy [. . .] Cobbett would have hailed Knightley as a paragon, the living embodiment of his 'resident *native* gentry' . . . Running the 'home-farm at Donwell', his everyday concerns are those of Cobbett's ideal, a proprietor 'attached to the soil'. His horses are for use on the farm, rarely to draw a carriage. He is ready to lecture Harriet Smith on 'modes of agriculture', to discuss with Robert Martin 'shows of cattle' and 'new drills' and to speak 'as a farmer' to his brother, reporting to John in fine detail 'what every field was to bear next year . . . the plan of a drain, the change of a fence, the felling of a tree, and the destination of every acre for wheat, turnips or spring corn'. Jane Austen's readers would recognize this as the language of agricultural improvement, of scientific farming, a professionalism regarded as fashionable and public-spirited under the royal patronage of 'Farmer' George and officially sponsored by the Board of Agriculture. To encourage self-sufficiency in the country's war-time food supplies, the Board commissioned a series of Agricultural Reports surveying farming practice county-by-county . . . Robert Martin, is an educated yeoman farmer who shares Knightley's progressive views and, pointedly, Jane Austen makes him a reader of the Agricultural Reports. [. . .]

Knightley is loyal to his heritage, intends that his patrimony should be passed on intact. Sensitive to the rights of the villagers, with their long established common rights, he chooses not even to re-route a path running across 'the home meadows . . . if it were to be the means of inconvenience to the Highbury people', a public-spiritedness which marks him out at the very time when land-owners were most heavily engaged in promoting acts of enclosure and blocking ancient rights-of-way.

From **Miranda J. Burgess, 'Austen, Radcliffe, and the Circulation of Britishness'**, in her *British Fiction and the Production of Social Order 1740–1830* (Cambridge: Cambridge University Press, 2000), pp. 150–64

> Miranda Burgess takes us back to Walter Scott's first review of *Emma* to show how Austen in renovating the 'romance' novel 'renovated Britain's history as well'. As a mother of the novel, Austen promoted the 'serious, dependable, and domestic, British to the bone' variety rather than the French novel of sensibility. Scott cast himself as Austen's inheritor and literary son and thereby 'for the first time, he granted literary history an explicitly national importance'.

Beginning with *Northanger Abbey*, written in 1797–8 but not published until 1818, Austen renovated romance. By marketing and circulating her reconditioned version of that markedly hybrid and historicized genre, she renovated Britain's history as well. The effects of her generic reconsiderations are noticeable even before their first publication in *Northanger Abbey*. While reviewing Austen's *Emma* for the *Quarterly Review* in 1815, Scott first drafted a formal pedigree for British fiction, establishing Austen's primacy as a mother of the novel. In keeping with the interests of the Tory *Quarterly*, he treated literary history as the consequence of a Burkean inheritance. Itself 'the legitimate child of the romance,' a French, courtly, extravagant though highly honourable form of fiction, the modern novel begot two children. One was the prodigal firstborn, whose descendants flourish in France, devoted to sensibility and to the dishonoured shade of the fantastic parent-form. The other, the cadet, is serious, dependable, and domestic, British to the bone. Its favourite children are Austen's works, the modern novel's legitimate, though late-born, inheritors. In 1832, in his Magnum Opus preface to *St. Ronan's Well*, Scott lent concreteness to this family history by recounting his own literary genealogy, casting himself as Austen's son and (implicitly) as the inheritor and improver of her literary dower. In so doing, for the first time, he granted literary history an explicitly national importance. [. . .]

[. . .] Whereas Scott worked from the homeland toward the home, Austen's novels, as Claudia Johnson argues, were directed from the private toward the national public sphere. It was by naming the new role Austen helped forge for romance as one of the movers and shakers of cultural history that Scott reconciled generic self-reflexion with his naturalized, avowedly evolutionary, and genetic legitimation of romance.

Austen, however, engaged in genre-reform of a different kind from Scott's, writing romances of British national identity without attempting to palliate or disguise any portion of the genre's or the nation's artifice. She confronted the problem that had faced patriotic conservatism since the economic and political upheavals of the 1790s: the suspicion that its conceptions of authority, history, and value in politics, letters, and the household were unnatural and therefore illegitimate. In her domestic novels, which are also national romances, Austen rested the full weight of legitimacy – not, like Hazlitt, on representation or consent; nor, like his opponent Burke, on virtue, chastity, and nature; nor even, like the Gothic revivalists Hurd, Gilpin, and Horace Walpole,[1] on Britain's native cultural inheritance – but on cultural construction: the artifice of romance itself. Threats of generic instability and 'illegitimacy' surface frequently in Austen's novels, most often as the *verso* side of parody. Her reformation of romance, seen retrospectively from the position of generic solidity romance achieved in part through her work, enabled Scott to naturalize literary history as the teleological result of a legitimate generic inheritance, rendering the descent of romance linear, uncontested, and smooth in the service of British nationhood.

The Work in Performance

There have been numerous film and television adaptations of Jane Austen. In the 1990s in particular there were highly successful adaptations of nearly all the novels, which raised her status to that of a Hollywood icon ('Who is this Jane Austen?' one studio executive reportedly asked, 'Can we get her to do a script for us?'). In the case of *Emma*, which had previously been adapted several times for the stage and dramatized for BBC television in 1972, there was both a made-for-television film (co-production of ITV in UK and A&E in USA, screenplay by the prolific British adapter of classic fiction Andrew Davies, starring Kate Beckinsale as Emma) and a cinema version (produced by Miramax, adapted and directed by Douglas McGrath, with Gwyneth Paltrow as Emma, Jeremy Northam as

---

1   Bishop Richard Hurd (1720–1808), whose *Letters on Chivalry and Romance* praised the native 'Gothic' or romance tradition of the medievals and Edmund Spenser above the classicism that dominated mid-eighteenth century literary culture; William Gilpin (1724–1804), pioneer of the cult of picturesque landscape; Horace Walpole (1717–97), letter writer, antiquarian, son of the influential statesman Robert Walpole, designer of an extraordinary Gothic house at Strawberry Hill and author of the first Gothic novel, *The Castle of Otranto* (1764).

Mr Knightley and Ewan McGregor as Frank Churchill). These and other film and television versions are discussed in a multi-authored collection of critical essays edited by Linda Troost and Sayre Greenfield entitled *Jane Austen in Hollywood* (Lexington: University Press of Kentucky, 1998).

The major problem for the literary adaptation of Austen's novels, and especially for *Emma*, is the rendering of the ironic third person narration, which is so crucial to the novel's effect. Many critics have accordingly suggested that the best adaptations are those that make radical departures from the original as a way of both finding visual equivalents for Austen's narrative voice and at the same time avoiding the 'heritage' feel of costume-drama that is reminiscent of the 'aunt Jane' Austenmania that thrived a century earlier. *Clueless* (Paramount Pictures, 1995, written and directed by Amy Heckerling, starring Alicia Silverstone) and *Mansfield Park* (joint production of Miramax and BBC Films, 1999, written and directed by Patricia Rozema) do something far more interesting than merely pay tribute to the genteel world of the novels. Rozema's *Mansfield Park* reflects an awareness of both postcolonial criticism (which has attended in detail to the source of Sir Thomas Bertram's wealth – his sugar plantation in Antigua) and gender criticism (the aura of sapphism that surrounds Mary Crawford). Rozema deftly weaves Austen's juvenilia and letters into the screenplay of the novel to stunning effect. The timid, sickly Fanny Price is represented as a version of Jane Austen herself, who occasionally breaks out into the wild girl of the juvenilia – 'do not faint, but run mad'. Austen's voice – of the novel, the letters and the juvenilia – is mediated by first-person voice-over.

The two orthodox films of *Emma* which appeared in 1996 – Andrew Davies's television version starring Kate Beckinsale in the title role and Douglas McGrath's lavish Hollywood film starring Gwyneth Paltrow – were fairly straightforward, faithful adaptations. Neither one managed to ironize fully their heroine, a flaw that strikes at the very heart of Austen's enterprise. Of course, the rendering of Austen's ironic voice is difficult to achieve in film, but Amy Heckerling succeeded in her inspired free adaptation of the previous year, *Clueless*,[1] which transposed the setting to Beverly Hills, but retained the theme of the moral awakening of a young girl (Emma herself becomes 'Cher', played to perfection by Alicia Silverstone). Heckerling adapted the novel to the modern period by clever updating. Instead of portraiture, there is photography; there are convertibles rather than carriages. Rather than the rarified and hierarchical world of Highbury, we have the privileged and socially stratified world of Beverly Hills, where so many of the teenagers are handsome, clever and rich. Mr Woodhouse's hypochondria becomes Cher's father's low cholesterol diet, the spinster Miss Bates is a lesbian gym teacher, and Frank Churchill's sexuality ineligibility is due to the fact that he is gay rather than secretly engaged. The illegitimate Harriet Smith character is a

---

1   The fact that the film was closely based on the plot and characterization of *Emma* was not mentioned in the credits and was not noticed by any reviewer on first release. But among Austen aficionados, word spread via the internet and there was subsequently considerable press discussion of the nature of the adaptation. Heckerling said that she was devoted to Jane Austen but did not want to put off a teenage audience by advertising the movie's 'high cultural' origins.

Latino transfer student, badly in need of a 'make-over'. The film works as a pastiche of the Hollywood teen movie, as well as an intelligent and hilarious take on *Emma*, which is closer in spirit to Jane Austen than any of the others.

From **Nora Nachumi, ' "As if!", Translating Austen's Ironic Narrator to Film'** (1998), in Linda Troost and Sayre Greenfield, eds, *Jane Austen in Hollywood* (Lexington, Ky.: University Press of Kentucky, 1998), pp. 130–9

> The key challenge for adapters of *Emma* is the rendering of the ironic third-person narrative. Nora Nachumi's essay shows how McGrath's film failed to ironize the heroine's faults, but how Heckerling achieved the art of being both inside and outside the character, so creating the right balance of sympathy and censure.

Granted that a movie need not be 'just like the book' in order to be good, there is a crucial problem in translating Austen's novels to film: what happens to the ironic, third-person narrative voice when Austen's novels are made into movies? [. . .]

Another aspect of McGrath's *Emma* substantially undermines the movie's efforts to portay the heroine in an ironic light . . . Paltrow's apparent perfection works against the notion that Emma must get off her pedestal and rejoin the human race. Despite her faults, this Emma ends the movie where she begins it, firmly fixed upon Mount Olympus. Indeed the movie works hard to deify Paltrow. She is lit to perfection. In interior scenes, she always seems to be in a little more light than the rest of the cast . . . as befits an Olympian, Paltrow is often dressed and posed like a Greek goddess [. . .]

[. . .] Thus, what could have been a *Bildungsroman* – a story of a young woman's education – ends up as a simple comedy of manners.

While McGrath's worship of Paltrow ultimately undermines the movie's original project, Amy Heckerling's *Clueless* faithfully replicates the ironic spirit of Austen's fifth novel. The protagonist Cher's skewed perspective and the role her environment plays in her misconceptions are dramatized by the contrast between her oh-so-literal narration and what we see on the screen. Her insistence, for example, that she is a normal teenager who gets dressed in the morning accompanies a vision of Cher in her dressing room coordinating outfits on a computer. Her matter-of-fact description of her mother's accidental death during a 'routine liposuction' identifies a terrifically tacky portrait of a woman with feathered hair. Later, Cher's need for a quiet place to relax introduces a shot of the shopping mall. In this manner, the film makes the relationship between the realities of Cher's environment and her self-absorbed image hilariously clear.

Although Heckerling's *Clueless* has been dismissed as a charming but 'light' version of Austen, *Clueless* is the only one of the three non-BBC films to recognize and replicate the most profound of *Emma*'s ironies. The genius of *Emma* is that it forces its readers to question the values and expectations they bring to the book. . . . Austen's irony thus functions on multiple levels. While Emma's 'mistakes' expose her own arrogance, they also open the door for a critique of those social conventions that deem a Harriet or Jane less of a 'catch' than a woman like Mrs Elton. Austen's irony, I think, encourages her readers to call into question those things we take for granted. If the fact that we misread the evidence suggests that we, like Emma, are shaped by the shape of our worlds, then Emma's awakening suggests that we also are able to consciously improve how we think and behave.

Although it tries, *Clueless* does not go this far. Unlike Frank's love for Jane, Christian's homosexuality is probably clear to most viewers long before it is apparent to Cher. As in McGrath's *Emma*, Cher's union with Josh is also obvious from the start. However, Cher's moral growth and her genuinely likable nature pose a challenge to those of us who harbor stereotypes about spoiled teenagers who live in Beverly Hills. More seriously, the film goes to great lengths to reinforce an image of Cher that it eventually dismantles. The first-person narration is extremely important to this endeavor because it makes Cher immensely appealing. It lets us know that a good heart beats within that shell of self-involved ignorance. The fact that Cher finally understands her own heart is – importantly – signaled by a newfound harmony between what she says and what we see on the screen. Like a giant cartoon lightbulb, a huge glowing fountain erupts in the background to signify the truth of Cher's revelation. Cher's new perspective is more than a realization about her feelings for Josh. She sees her old behavior as shallow, and this gives her the power to alter her world. There is no question that *Sense and Sensibility* is a less 'silly' book than *Clueless* a movie. But, in its own charming way, *Clueless* encourages its viewers to 'makeover their souls.'

3

Key passages

Introduction

'I am going to take a heroine whom no one but myself will much like.'[1]

Jane Austen was well aware of the gamble she was taking in depicting a heroine who is essentially flawed, and who, for most of the narrative, gets so much wrong. Austen complained heartily about the tendency of her fellow novelists to portray flawless and unrealistic heroines, 'Pictures of perfection make me sick and wicked'.[2] Though determined to avoid this convention, she was aware she would have problems in maintaining the reader's sympathy for Emma. Austen's way of getting around this problem led to a bold and pioneering narrative technique: the use of ironic third-person narration, sometimes called 'free indirect speech'. The text creates the illusion of being written from the point of view of the individual character, but the distance of the author is maintained. This device enables Austen to be both inside and outside her character; she keeps the viewpoint close to Emma's in order to ensure our sympathetic identification with her, but at the same time ironizes her from a distance, showing how she gets things wrong. Austen had used this very complex and highly effective method of narration in her previous novels, but not to the extent that she did with *Emma*.

---

1   James Edward Austen-Leigh, *A Memoir of Jane Austen and Other Family Recollections* [1870], ed. and introduced by Kathryn Sutherland (Oxford: Oxford University Press, 2002).
2   *Letters*, p. 335.

Key Passages

Volume 1, Chapter 1

The main characters and themes are introduced with great economy and precision. Emma's mother has died in her early childhood, and Miss Taylor, who has been Emma's governess and friend, has married a widower, Mr Weston. Emma lives with her elderly father, whilst her sister Isabella is married and settled in London. The Woodhouses are established as an important, wealthy family in the village of Highbury. The other character that we meet is Mr Knightley, a family friend and relation (he is the brother of Isabella's husband).

The first half of the opening chapter is written from the third-person omniscient point of view. The author establishes the setting of the village of Highbury, and the status of the Woodhouse family as 'first in consequence there'. We are told that Emma's mother died a long time ago, and her sister has married, leaving her mistress of Hartfield. The heroine is described in the opening sentence as 'handsome, clever and rich'. Up until this point in her life she has had 'very little to distress or vex her'. The loss of Emma's former governess, and friend, Miss Taylor, is presented as the first important change in Emma's life, leaving her in 'intellectual solitude'. Though Miss Taylor has supplied a mother's affection, she has imposed little 'restraint' or control over her charge. As a consequence, Emma has had 'rather too much of her own way', and has a 'disposition to think a little too well of herself'. The authorial voice is warning the reader that though this is a heroine who appears to be perfect on the surface, she is, in fact, rather spoilt and conceited and possibly heading for a fall. Thus before we hear Emma's own voice, we are prepared for a flawed heroine who 'seemed [my italics] to unite some of the best blessings of existence'.

Emma Woodhouse, handsome, clever, and rich, with a comfortable home and happy disposition, seemed to unite some of the best blessings of existence; and had lived nearly twenty-one years in the world with very little to distress or vex her.

She was the youngest of the two daughters of a most affectionate, indulgent father, and had, in consequence of her sister's marriage, been mistress of his house from a very early period. Her mother had died too long ago for her to have more than an indistinct remembrance of her caresses, and her place had been supplied by an excellent woman as governess, who had fallen little short of a mother in affection.

Sixteen years had Miss Taylor been in Mr Woodhouse's family, less as a governess than a friend, very fond of both daughters, but particularly of Emma. Between *them* it was more the intimacy of sisters. Even before Miss Taylor had ceased to hold the nominal office of governess, the mildness of her temper had hardly allowed her to impose any restraint; and the shadow of authority being now long passed away, they had been living together as friend and friend very mutually attached, and Emma doing just what she liked; highly esteeming Miss Taylor's judgment, but directed chiefly by her own.

The real evils indeed of Emma's situation were the power of having rather too much her own way, and a disposition to think a little too well of herself; these were the disadvantages which threatened alloy to her many enjoyments. The danger, however, was at present so unperceived, that they did not by any means rank as misfortunes with her.

Sorrow came – a gentle sorrow – but not at all in the shape of any disagreeable consciousness. – Miss Taylor married. It was Miss Taylor's loss which first brought grief. [. . .]

How was she to bear the change? – It was true that her friend was going only half a mile from them; but Emma was aware that great must be the difference between a Mrs Weston only half a mile from them, and a Miss Taylor in the house; and with all her advantages, natural and domestic, she was now in great danger of suffering from intellectual solitude. She dearly loved her father, but he was no companion for her. He could not meet her in conversation, rational or playful.

The evil of the actual disparity in their ages (and Mr Woodhouse had not married early) was much increased by his constitution and habits; for having been a valetudinarian[3] all his life, without activity of mind or body, he was a much older man in ways than in years; and though everywhere beloved for the friendliness of his heart and his amiable temper, his talents could not have recommended him at any time.

Her sister, though comparatively but little removed by matrimony, being settled in London, only sixteen miles off, was much beyond her daily reach; and many a long October and November evening must be struggled through at Hartfield, before Christmas brought the next visit from Isabella and her husband and their little children to fill the house and give her pleasant society again.

Highbury, the large and populous village almost amounting to a town, to which Hartfield, in spite of its separate lawn and shrubberies and name, did really belong, afforded her no equals. The Woodhouses were first in consequence there.

---

3   A person of poor health or unduly anxious about health. Mr Woodhouse is also concerned about
    the health of others, particularly the women (see **pp. 82–3**).

All looked up to them. She had many acquaintance in the place, for her father was universally civil, but not one among them who could be accepted in lieu of Miss Taylor for even half a day.

The second half of the chapter is rendered mainly in dialogue form between Emma, Mr Woodhouse and Mr Knightley, with very little authorial commentary. Emma and her father discuss family matters. Though Emma is distressed by the loss of her friend, she comforts Mr Woodhouse, and attempts to raise his spirits. Despite her faults, she is devoted to her father. Note how they speak about their servants as family members and address them by their Christian names, unlike Mrs Elton who forgets the names of her servants and treats them as inferiors.

The dialogue between Emma and Mr Knightley reveals the nature of their friendship. Their playful banter suggests a relationship of intellectual equals; they tease each other and are witty and clever. They are very good friends, and have no illusions about each other. Mr Woodhouse, by contrast, is slow-witted and child-like.

The chain of events arising from the loss of Miss Taylor, which leaves Emma to her own devices, has been initiated by Emma's matchmaking. Even though Mr Knightley and Mr Woodhouse disapprove of this activity, Emma is determined to carry on. She reveals that she has decided to find a wife for clergyman, Mr Elton. Mr Knightley ends the chapter with his witty remark: 'help him to the best of the fish and the chicken, but leave him to chuse his own wife'.

'My dear, how am I to get so far? Randalls is such a distance. I could not walk half so far.'

'No, papa, nobody thought of your walking. We must go in the carriage to be sure.'

'The carriage! But James will not like to put the horses to for such a little way; – and where are the poor horses to be while we are paying our visit?'

'They are to be put into Mr Weston's stable, papa. You know we have settled all that already. We talked it all over with Mr Weston last night. And as for James, you may be very sure he will always like going to Randalls, because of his daughter's being housemaid there. I only doubt whether he will ever take us anywhere else. That was your doing, Papa. You got Hannah that good place. Nobody thought of Hannah till you mentioned her – James is so obliged to you!' [. . .]

Mr Knightley, a sensible man about seven or eight-and-thirty, was not only a very old and intimate friend of the family, but particularly connected with it as the elder brother of Isabella's husband. He lived about a mile from Highbury, was a frequent visitor and always welcome, and at this time more welcome than usual, as coming directly from their mutual connections in London. [. . .]

'It is very kind of you, Mr Knightley, to come out at this late hour to call upon us. I am afraid you must have had a shocking walk.'

'Not at all, sir. It is a beautiful, moonlight night; and so mild that I must draw back from your great fire.'

'But you must have found it very damp and dirty. I wish you may not catch cold.'

'Dirty, sir! Look at my shoes. Not a speck on them.'

'Well! That is quite surprising, for we have had a vast deal of rain here. It rained dreadfully hard for half an hour, while we were at breakfast. I wanted them to put off the wedding.'

'By the bye – I have not wished you joy. Being pretty well aware of what sort of joy you must both be feeling, I have been in no hurry with my congratulations. But I hope it all went off tolerably well. How did you all behave? Who cried most?'

'Ah! Poor Miss Taylor! 'tis a sad business.'

'Poor Mr and Miss Woodhouse, if you please; but I cannot possibly say "poor Miss Taylor". I have a great regard for you and Emma; but when it comes to the question of dependence or independence! – At any rate, it must be better to have only one to please, than two.'

'Especially when *one* of those two is such a fanciful, troublesome creature!' said Emma playfully. 'That is what you have in your head, I know – and what you would certainly say if my father were not by.'

'I believe it is very true, my dear, indeed,' said Mr Woodhouse with a sigh. 'I am afraid I am sometimes very fanciful and troublesome.'

'My dearest papa! You do not think I could mean *you*, or suppose Mr Knightley to mean *you*. What a horrible idea! Oh, no! I meant only myself. Mr Knightley loves to find fault with me you know – in a joke – it is all a joke. We always say what we like to one another.'

Mr Knightley, in fact, was one of the few people who could see faults in Emma Woodhouse, and the only one who ever told her of them: and though this was not particularly agreeable to Emma herself, she knew it would be so much less so to her father, that she would not have him really suspect such a circumstance as her not being thought perfect by every body. [. . .]

'And you have forgotten one matter of joy to me,' said Emma, 'and a very considerable one – that I made the match myself. I made the match, you know, four years ago; and to have it take place, and be proved in the right, when so many people said Mr Weston would never marry again, may comfort me for any thing.'

Mr Knightley shook his head at her. Her father fondly replied, 'Ah, my dear, I wish you would not make matches and fortel things, for whatever you say always comes to pass. Pray do not make any more matches.'

'I promise you to make none for myself, papa; but I must, indeed, for other people. It is the greatest amusement in the world! [. . .] you cannot think, I shall leave off match-making [. . .] Only one more, papa; only for Mr Elton. Poor Mr Elton! You like Mr Elton, papa, – I must look about for a wife for him. There is nobody in Highbury who deserves him – and he has been here a whole year, and has fitted up his house so comfortably that it would be a shame to have him single any longer – and I thought when he was joining their hands to-day, he looked so very much as if he would like to have the same kind of office done for him! I think very well of Mr Elton, and this is the only way I have of doing him a service.'

'Mr Elton is a very pretty young man to be sure, and a very good young man, and I have a great regard for him. But if you want to shew him any attention, my dear, ask him to come and dine with us some day. That will be a much better thing. I dare say Mr Knightley will be so kind as to meet him.'

'With a great deal of pleasure, sir, at any time,' said Mr Knightley laughing; 'and I agree with you entirely that it will be a much better thing. Invite him to dinner, Emma, and help him to the best of the fish and the chicken, but leave him to chuse his own wife. Depend upon it, a man of six or seven-and-twenty can take care of himself.'

Volume 1, Chapter 3

Mrs Bates, 'the widow of a former vicar of Highbury', lives with her spinster daughter in reduced circumstances. Despite her poverty, Miss Bates is a much-loved figure in the village, and does not conform to the stereotype of the unhappy spinster described by Emma to Harriet. Mr Knightley later says of her, 'She is a standing lesson of how to be happy'. Jane Austen gives little in the way of physical descriptions of her characters, and Miss Bates's character is mainly rendered through the quasi-dramatic force of her monologues. Nevertheless, the authorial reflections on Miss Bates's lack of 'intellectual superiority to make atonement to herself' has attracted commentary from critics who object to the harshness of Austen's perspective (see **p. 53**). Other critics have viewed Miss Bates as a central figure who unites all the different scions of Highbury (see **pp. 68–9, 87**).

Mrs Bates, the widow of a former vicar of Highbury, was a very old lady, almost past every thing but tea and quadrille.[1] She lived with her single daughter in a very small way, and was considered with all the regard and respect which a harmless old lady, under such untoward circumstances, can excite. Her daughter enjoyed a most uncommon degree of popularity for a woman neither young, handsome, rich, nor married. Miss Bates stood in the very worst predicament in the world for having much of the public favour; and she had no intellectual superiority to make atonement to herself, or frighten those who might hate her, into outward respect. She had never boasted either beauty or cleverness. Her youth had passed without distinction, and her middle of life was devoted to the care of a failing mother, and the endeavour to make a small income go as far as possible. And yet she was a happy woman, and a woman whom no one named without good-will. It was her own universal good-will and contented temper which worked such wonders. She loved every body, was interested in every body's happiness, quick-sighted to every body's merits; thought herself a most fortunate creature, and surrounded with

---

1 A card game for four players with forty cards.

blessings in such an excellent mother and so many good neighbours and friends, and a home that wanted for nothing. The simplicity and cheerfulness of her nature, her contented and grateful spirit, were a recommendation to every body and a mine of felicity to herself. She was a great talker upon little matters, which exactly suited Mr Woodhouse, full of trivial communications and harmless gossip.

It is rare for Austen to give a physical description of her characters, yet Harriet is described in some detail. Her appearance is rendered from Emma's snobbish point of view: 'Those soft blue eyes and all those natural graces should not be wasted on the inferior society of Highbury and its connections'. Emma's interest in Harriet's physical beauty has led some critics to ponder on the heroine's possible homosexual inclinations (see **p. 55**). Emma is now taking on the role of tutor; as Miss Taylor has nurtured Emma, so she will nurture Harriet.

The first part of the passage is a straightforward description of Harriet's position in society. She is an illegitimate child, with few connections. However, the second part of the passage is rendered through 'free indirect speech', the ironic, third-person narrative technique that allows Austen to be both inside and outside her character. It is Emma who decides that Harriet must be introduced into 'good society' and detached from 'bad acquaintance'. Note how Emma's voice differs from the objective voice of the narrator, and how it belies the information we receive from the narrator. An illegitimate child in Austen's society has no status, yet Emma raises her Harriet to an absurdly high level in her belief that she is above the 'inferior' society of Highbury. Furthermore, behind Emma's misguided notion of improving her friend is self-aggrandisement. Harriet pleases because she shows a 'proper and becoming deference' to Emma, which asserts her own social importance. Even if Harriet becomes Emma's friend, she will still be considered inferior to her. Austen invites us to consider the authenticity of Emma's 'kind undertaking' to improve Harriet.

Harriet Smith was the natural daughter of somebody. Somebody had placed her, several years back, at Mrs Goddard's school, and somebody had lately raised her from the condition of scholar to that of parlour-boarder. This was all that was generally known of her history. She had no visible friends but what had been acquired at Highbury, and was now just returned from a long visit in the country to some young ladies who had been at school there with her.

She was a very pretty girl, and her beauty happened to be of a sort which Emma particularly admired. She was short, plump and fair, with a fine bloom, blue eyes, light hair, regular features, and a look of great sweetness; and before the end of the evening, Emma was as much pleased with her manners as her person, and quite determined to continue the acquaintance.

She was not struck by any thing remarkably clever in Miss Smith's conversation, but she found her altogether very engaging – not inconveniently shy, not unwilling to talk – and yet so far from pushing, shewing so proper and becoming a deference, seeming so pleasantly grateful for being admitted to Hartfield, and so artlessly impressed by the appearance of every thing in so superior a style to what she had been used to, that she must have good sense and deserve encouragement. Encouragement should be given. Those soft blue eyes and all those natural graces should not be wasted on the inferior society of Highbury and its connections. The acquaintance she had already formed were unworthy of her. The friends from whom she had just parted, though very good sort of people, must be doing her harm. They were a family of the name of Martin, whom Emma well knew by character, as renting a large farm of Mr Knightley, and residing in the parish of Donwell – very creditably she believed – she knew Mr Knightley thought highly of them – but they must be coarse and unpolished, and very unfit to be the intimates of a girl who wanted only a little more knowledge and elegance to be quite perfect. *She* would notice her; she would improve her; she would detach her from her bad acquaintance, and introduce her into good society; she would form her opinions and her manners. It would be an interesting, and certainly a very kind undertaking; highly becoming her own situation in life, her leisure, and powers.

Volume 1, Chapter 5

In this chapter, Mr Knightley and Mrs Weston discuss Emma. Mr Knightley argues that Emma's friendship with Harriet is bad for her because it confirms Emma's sense of her own importance. He is also concerned that Harriet will feel displaced and uncomfortable in her new social sphere. They discuss Emma's beauty and vigour – she is 'the picture of health'. Some critics have analysed the importance of health and disease in the novel (see **p. 82**). Mr Knightley and Mrs Weston are both tutor figures to Emma, although Mr Knightley has a clearer sense of her faults. Feminist critic Claudia Johnson has suggested, however, that Mrs Weston's belief in Emma's essential integrity is eventually vindicated: 'she has qualities which may be trusted; she will never lead any one really wrong; she will make no lasting blunder' (see **p. 80**).

'Emma is spoiled by being the cleverest of her family . . . and ever since she was twelve, Emma has been mistress of the house and of you all. In her mother she lost the only person able to cope with her. She inherits her mother's talents, and must have been under subjection to her.' [. . .]

[. . .] 'But Harriet Smith – I have not half done about Harriet Smith. I think her the very worst sort of companion that Emma could possibly have. She knows nothing herself, and looks upon Emma as knowing every thing. She is a flatterer in all her ways; and so much the worse, because undesigned. Her ignorance is hourly flattery. How can Emma imagine she has any thing to learn herself, while Harriet is presenting such a delightful inferiority? And as for Harriet, I will venture to say that *she* cannot gain by the acquaintance. Hartfield will only put her out of conceit with all the other places she belongs to. She will grow just refined enough to be uncomfortable with those among whom birth and circumstances have placed her home. I am much mistaken if Emma's doctrines give any strength of mind, or tend at all to make a girl adapt herself rationally to the varieties of her situation in life. – They only give a little polish.'

'I either depend more upon Emma's good sense than you do, or am more anxious for her present comfort; for I cannot lament the acquaintance. How well she looked last night!'

'Oh! you would rather talk of her person than her mind, would you? Very well; I shall not attempt to deny Emma's being pretty.'

'Pretty! say beautiful rather. Can you imagine any thing nearer perfect beauty than Emma altogether – face and figure?'

'I do not know what I could imagine, but I confess that I have seldom seen a face or figure more pleasing to me than her's. But I am a partial old friend.'

'Such an eye! – the true hazle eye – and so brilliant! regular features, open countenance, with a complexion! oh! what a bloom of full health, and such a pretty height and size; such a firm and upright figure. There is health, not merely in her bloom, but in her air, her head, her glance. One hears sometimes of a child being "the picture of health;" now Emma always gives me the idea of being the complete picture of grown-up health. She is loveliness itself. Mr Knightley, is not she?'

'I have not a fault to find with her person,' he replied. 'I think her all you describe. I love to look at her; and I will add this praise, that I do not think her personally vain. Considering how very handsome she is, she appears to be little occupied with it; her vanity lies another way. Mrs Weston, I am not to be talked out of my dislike of her intimacy with Harriet Smith, or my dread of its doing them both harm.'

'And I, Mr Knightley, am equally stout in my confidence of its not doing them any harm. With all dear Emma's little faults, she is an excellent creature. Where shall we see a better daughter, or a kinder sister, or a truer friend? No, no; she has qualities which may be trusted; she will never lead any one really wrong; she will make no lasting blunder; where Emma errs once, she is in the right a hundred times.'

Volume 1, Chapter 6

Emma continues to foster the relationship between Harriet and Mr Elton, without realizing that she is herself the object of Elton's interest. This is an example of Austen's comic irony; the means by which she enables the reader to perceive that Emma's skewed version of reality is different to the 'real one'. The reader's intelligence is duly flattered as one feels that one knows what is 'really' going on. The confusion surrounding the portrait of Harriet is indicative of Emma's tendency to misunderstand events around her. She misinterprets Elton's effusive compliments to her as a mark of his gratitude 'on Harriet's account'.

'Let me entreat you,' cried Mr Elton . . . 'to exercise so charming a talent in favour of your friend. I know what your drawings are. How could you suppose me ignorant? Is not this room rich in specimens of your landscapes and flowers; and has not Mrs Weston some inimitable figure-pieces in her drawing-room at Randalls?'

Yes, good man! – thought Emma – but what has all that to do with taking likenesses? You know nothing of drawing. Don't pretend to be in raptures about mine. Keep your raptures for Harriet's face' [. . .]

'You, sir, may say any thing,' cried Mr Elton; 'but I must confess that I regard it as a most happy thought, the placing of Miss Smith out of doors; and the tree is touched with such inimitable spirit! Any other situation would have been much less in character. The naïveté of Miss Smith's manners – and altogether – Oh, it is most admirable! I cannot keep my eyes from it. I never saw such a likeness.'

The next thing wanted was to get the picture framed; and here were a few difficulties. It must be done directly; it must be done in London; the order must go through the hands of some intelligent person whose taste could be depended on; and Isabella, the usual doer of all commissions, must not be applied to, because it was December, and Mr Woodhouse could not bear the idea of her stirring out of her house in the fogs of December. But no sooner was the distress known to Mr Elton, than it was removed. His gallantry was always on the alert. 'Might he be trusted with the commission, what infinite pleasure should he have in executing it! he could ride to London at any time. It was impossible to say how much he should be gratified by being employed on such an errand.'

'He was too good! – she could not endure the thought! – she would not give him such a troublesome office for the world' – brought on the desired repetition of entreaties and assurances, – and a very few minutes settled the business.

Mr Elton was to take the drawing to London, chuse the frame, and give the directions; and Emma thought she could so pack it as to ensure its safety without much incommoding him, while he seemed mostly fearful of not being incommoded enough.

'What a precious deposit!' said he with a tender sigh, as he received it.

'This man is almost too gallant to be in love,' thought Emma. 'I should say so, but that I suppose there may be a hundred different ways of being in love. He is an excellent young man, and will suit Harriet exactly; it will be an "Exactly so," as he says himself; but he does sigh and languish, and study for compliments rather more than I could endure as a principal. I come in for a pretty good share as a second. But it is his gratitude on Harriet's account.'

Volume 1, Chapter 7

Harriet receives a proposal of marriage from the man she loves, Mr Martin, and Emma persuades her to reject it, encouraging Harriet to believe that she is in love with Mr Elton.

Emma's interference in Harriet's life is shown to have increasingly serious consequences. Emma is portrayed in a very unflattering light as she plays on her friend's weak intellect to persuade her to refuse a very worthy marriage proposal. Emma's generalizations about the Martins reveal her to be a potentially dangerous snob and we see how she abuses her power in her manipulation of Harriet. Jane Austen often uses letters to reveal character, and Martin's intelligence and worthiness are reflected in Emma's (reluctant) approval of his 'vigorous and decided' style. Yet despite her better judgement, she persuades her friend to refuse him. In Austen's early comic novel 'Love and Freindship' [sic], the anti-heroines, Laura and Sophia, ruin the life of their friend by persuading her to elope with a fortune hunter (see **p. 20**). Emma's interference in a young girl's happiness is similarly destructive and egotistic: 'I could not have visited Mrs Robert Martin, of Abbey-Mill Farm. Now I am secure of you for ever'.

Note also the irony contained in Emma's advice to Harriet: 'There is no danger of your not being intelligible, which is the first thing. Your meaning must be unequivocal.' Throughout the novel, Austen exploits the unequivocal, the ambiguous and the unintelligible. Emma's comments are rich in dramatic irony, which reveal the extent of her self-deception. She warns her friend, 'Harriet, do not deceive yourself', although it is Emma who deceives herself. Emma's extreme self-delusion is also revealed in her comment: 'While you were at all in suspense I kept my feelings to myself, but now that you are so completely decided I have no hesitation in approving.'

Although the scene is rendered mainly in dialogue, Austen also uses free indirect speech to ironize her heroine. For example, the line 'the symptoms were favourable' appears to be a statement made by an impersonal author, but in act it is an expression of Emma's private thoughts. This is a good example of the filtering of the narrative through the heroine's consciousness. The reader realizes that Emma is manipulating Harriet for her own ends.

'Upon my word,' she cried, 'the young man is determined not to lose any thing for want of asking. He will connect himself well if he can.'

'Will you read the letter?' cried Harriet. 'Pray do. I'd rather you would.'

Emma was not sorry to be pressed. She read, and was surprised. The style of the letter was much above her expectation. There were not merely no grammatical errors, but as a composition it would not have disgraced a gentleman; the language, though plain, was strong and unaffected, and the sentiments it conveyed very much to the credit of the writer. It was short, but expressed good sense, warm attachment, liberality, propriety, even delicacy of feeling. She paused over it, while Harriet stood anxiously watching for her opinion, with a 'Well, well,' and was at last forced to add, 'Is it a good letter? or is it too short?'

'Yes, indeed, a very good letter,' replied Emma rather slowly – 'so good a letter, Harriet, that every thing considered, I think one of his sisters must have helped him. I can hardly imagine the young man whom I saw talking with you the other day could express himself so well, if left quite to his own powers, and yet it is not the style of a woman; no, certainly, it is too strong and concise; not diffuse enough for a woman. No doubt he is a sensible man, and I suppose may have a natural talent for – thinks strongly and clearly – and when he takes a pen in hand, his thoughts naturally find proper words. It is so with some men. Yes, I understand the sort of mind. Vigorous, decided, with sentiments to a certain point, not coarse. A better written letter, Harriet, (returning it,) than I had expected.'

'Well,' said the still waiting Harriet; – 'well – and – and what shall I do?'

'What shall you do! In what respect? Do you mean with regard to this letter?'

'Yes.'

'But what are you in doubt of? You must answer it of course – and speedily.'

'Yes. But what shall I say? Dear Miss Woodhouse, do advise me.'

'Oh, no, no! the letter had much better be all your own. You will express yourself very properly, I am sure. There is no danger of your not being intelligible, which is the first thing. Your meaning must be unequivocal; no doubts or demurs . . .'

'[. . .] – but if you would just advise me what I had best do – No, no, I do not mean that – As you say, one's mind ought to be quite made up – One should not be hesitating – It is a very serious thing. – It will be safer to say "No", perhaps. – Do you think I had better say "No?" '

'Not for the world,' said Emma, smiling graciously, 'would I advise you either way. You must be the best judge of your own happiness. If you prefer Mr Martin to every other person; if you think him the most agreeable man you have ever been in company with, why should you hesitate? You blush, Harriet. – Does any body else occur to you at this moment under such a definition? Harriet, Harriet, do not deceive yourself; do not be run away with by gratitude and compassion. At this moment whom are you thinking of?'

The symptoms were favourable. – Instead of answering, Harriet turned away confused, and stood thoughtfully by the fire; and though the letter was still in her hand, it was now mechanically twisted about without regard. Emma waited the result with impatience, but not without strong hopes. At last, with some hesitation, Harriet said–

'Miss Woodhouse, as you will not give me your opinion, I must do as well as I can by myself; and I have now quite determined, and really almost made up my mind – to refuse Mr Martin. Do you think I am right?'

'Perfectly, perfectly right, my dearest Harriet; you are doing just what you ought. While you were at all in suspense I kept my feelings to myself, but now that you are so completely decided I have no hesitation in approving. Dear Harriet, I give myself joy of this. It would have grieved me to lose your acquaintance, which must have been the consequence of your marrying Mr Martin. While you were in the smallest degree wavering, I said nothing about it, because I would not influence; but it would have been the loss of a friend to me. I could not have visited Mrs Robert Martin, of Abbey-Mill Farm. Now I am secure of you for ever.'

Volume 1, Chapter 8

Mr Knightley and Emma discuss Harriet's marriage proposal, and Emma is shown to be even more in error as she insists that Robert Martin is unworthy of her friend.

Emma's lack of judgement is most apparent in her opinions of Mr Elton and Robert Martin. Her conviction that the handsome and gallant Mr Elton is a 'model' of good manners is as wrong-headed as her observation of Robert Martin's 'clownish' manners. Emma's snobbish and absurd comment that Robert Martin is 'not Harriet's equal' is angrily quashed by Mr Knightley: 'No, he is not her equal indeed, for he is as much her superior in sense as in situation'. Whilst Emma thinks of compatibility in terms of rank and station, Mr Knightley puts his emphasis on compatibility of mind and disposition. In contrast to Emma, Mr Knightley has a clear sense of Harriet's social position. He makes the point that Emma is 'blinded' by her 'infatuation' with Harriet, and that Harriet has few qualities of her own to secure a respectable marriage. Mr Knightley rates intelligence and good sense above other considerations, and is harsh in his treatment of Harriet, a view he will later modify: 'A degradation to illegitimacy and ignorance, to be married to a respectable, intelligent gentleman-farmer!' Emma's views are shown to be both erroneous and snobbish: 'The sphere in which she moves is much above his. – It would be a degradation.' She also has romantic notions about Harriet's origins, which are clearly not shared by Mr Knightley. Such is her faith in Harriet's true gentility that she fires a parting shot that will later rebound upon her: 'Were you, yourself, ever to marry, she is the very woman for you'.

The passage is rendered in dialogue, and Mr Knightley is given the role of moral censurer. He is the only character who openly points out Emma's errors and shows her her faults. He also has few illusions about her, quickly realizing that it was Emma who wrote Harriet's rejection letter. He also perceives that Emma's motives in respect to Harriet are self-serving: 'She had no sense of superiority then. If she has it now, you have given it. You have been no friend to Harriet Smith, Emma.'

'Pray, Mr Knightley,' said Emma, who had been smiling to herself through a great part of this speech, 'how do you know that Mr Martin did not speak yesterday?'

'Certainly,' replied he, surprized, 'I do not absolutely know it; but it may be inferred. Was not she the whole day with you?'

'Come,' said she, 'I will tell you something, in return for what you have told me. He did speak yesterday – that is, he wrote, and was refused.'

This was obliged to be repeated before it could be believed; and Mr Knightley actually looked red with surprize and displeasure, as he stood up, in tall indignation, and said,

'Then she is a greater simpleton than I ever believed her. What is the foolish girl about?'

'Oh! to be sure,' cried Emma, 'it is always incomprehensible to a man that a woman should ever refuse an offer of marriage. A man always imagines a woman to be ready for anybody who asks her.'

'Nonsense! a man does not imagine any such thing. But what is the meaning of this? Harriet Smith refuse Robert Martin? madness, if it is so; but I hope you are mistaken.'

'I saw her answer, nothing could be clearer.'

'You saw her answer! you wrote her answer too. Emma, this is your doing. You persuaded her to refuse him.'

'And if I did, (which, however, I am far from allowing,) I should not feel that I had done wrong. Mr Martin is a very respectable young man, but I cannot admit him to be Harriet's equal; and am rather surprized indeed that he should have ventured to address her. By your account, he does seem to have had some scruples. It is a pity that they were ever got over.'

'Not Harriet's equal!' exclaimed Mr Knightley loudly and warmly; and with calmer asperity, added, a few moments afterwards, 'No, he is not her equal indeed, for he is as much her superior in sense as in situation. Emma, your infatuation about that girl blinds you. What are Harriet Smith's claims, either of birth, nature or education, to any connection higher than Robert Martin? She is the natural daughter of nobody knows whom, with probably no settled provision at all, and certainly no respectable relations. She is known only as parlour-boarder at a common school. She is not a sensible girl, nor a girl of any information. She has been taught nothing useful, and is too young and too simple to have acquired any thing herself. At her age she can have no experience, and with her little wit, is not very likely ever to have any that can avail her. She is pretty, and she is good tempered, and that is all. My only scruple in advising the match was on his account, as being beneath his deserts, and a bad connexion for him. I felt, that as to fortune, in all probability he might do much better; and that as to a rational companion or useful helpmate, he could not do worse. But I could not reason so to a man in love, and was willing to trust to there being no harm in her, to her having that sort of disposition, which, in good hands, like his, might be easily led aright and turn out very well. The advantage of the match I felt to be all on her side; and had not the smallest doubt (nor have I now) that there would be a general cry-out upon her extreme good luck. Even *your* satisfaction I made sure of. It crossed my mind immediately that you would not regret your friend's leaving Highbury, for the sake of her being settled so well. I remember saying to myself, "Even Emma, with all her partiality for Harriet, will think this a good match." '

'I cannot help wondering at your knowing so little of Emma as to say any such thing. What! think a farmer, (and with all his sense and all his merit Mr Martin is nothing more,) a good match for my intimate friend! Not regret her leaving Highbury for the sake of marrying a man whom I could never admit as an acquaintance of my own! I wonder you should think it possible for me to have such feelings. I assure you mine are very different. I must think your statement by no means fair. You are not just to Harriet's claims. They would be estimated very differently by others as well as myself; Mr Martin may be the richest of the two, but he is undoubtedly her inferior as to rank in society. – The sphere in which she moves is much above his. – It would be a degradation.'

'A degradation to illegitimacy and ignorance, to be married to a respectable, intelligent gentleman-farmer!'

'As to the circumstances of her birth, though in a legal sense she may be called Nobody, it will not hold in common sense. She is not to pay for the offence of others, by being held below the level of those with whom she is brought up. – There can scarcely be a doubt that her father is a gentleman – and a gentleman of fortune. – Her allowance is very liberal; nothing has ever been grudged for her improvement or comfort. – That she is a gentleman's daughter, is indubitable to me; that she associates with gentlemen's daughters, no one, I apprehend, will deny. – She is superior to Mr Robert Martin.'

'Whoever might be her parents,' said Mr Knightley, 'whoever may have had the charge of her, it does not appear to have been any part of their plan to introduce her into what you would call good society. After receiving a very indifferent education she is left in Mrs Goddard's hands to shift as she can; – to move, in short, in Mrs Goddard's line, to have Mrs Goddard's acquaintance. Her friends evidently thought this good enough for her; and it *was* good enough. She desired nothing better herself. Till you chose to turn her into a friend, her mind had no distaste for her own set, nor any ambition beyond it. She was as happy as possible with the Martins in the summer. She had no sense of superiority then. If she has it now, you have given it. You have been no friend to Harriet Smith, Emma. [. . .] to hear you abusing the reason you have [. . .] better to be without sense, than misapply it as you do.'

'To be sure!', cried she playfully [. . .] 'I know that such a girl as Harriet is exactly what every man delights in . . . Were you, yourself, ever to marry, she is the very woman for you.'

Volume 1, Chapter 9

In preference to reading, the only 'literary pursuit' that Harriet is capable of is making a collection of riddles. Mr Elton is persuaded to contribute one, which is left for the reader to guess (the answer is 'woe-man'). Many post-modern scholars have picked up on the riddles and charades that the reader is left to decode (see **pp. 83–4**). The riddles and word games also reflect the ambiguities and misunderstandings of the Elton/Harriet/Emma triangle. A riddle has either a right or a wrong answer, and just as Emma gets it wrong with Mr Elton, so too can the reader on a first reading of *Emma*. Some critics have compared the novel to a detective story which is only fully clarified by a second reading (see **p. 33**). Thus Austen exploits the ambiguities of her plot to create further twists and comic misunderstandings, which have further ironic resonances on repeated readings of the novel. Later in the chapter, when Emma returns the charade to Elton, he 'glanced at Emma and at Harriet'. Here, the reader can be forgiven for making the same mistake as Emma, and the comic irony is less easy to distinguish. But on a second reading, the reader realizes that Elton's attentions are directed solely at Emma, and the comedy is enriched.

Her views of improving her little friend's mind, by a great deal of useful reading and conversation, had never yet led to more than a few first chapters, and the intention of going on tomorrow. It was much easier to chat than to study [. . .] and the only literary pursuit which engaged Harriet at present, the only mental provision she was making for the evening of life, was the collecting and transcribing all the riddles of every sort that she could meet with, into a thin quarto of hot-pressed paper, made up by her friend, and ornamented with ciphers and trophies [. . .]

[Mr Elton] was invited to contribute any really good enigmas, charades or conundrums that he might recollect . . . They owed to him their two or three politest puzzles; and the joy and exultation with which at last he recalled, and rather sentimentally recited, that well-known charade,

> My first doth affliction denote,
> Which my second is destin'd to feel
> And my whole is the best antidote
> That affliction to soften and heal. –

made her quite sorry to acknowledge that they had transcribed it some pages ago already.

'Why will not you write one yourself for us, Mr Elton?' said she; 'that is the only security for its freshness; and nothing could be easier to you.'

'Oh, no! he had never written, hardly ever, any thing of the kind in his life. The stupidest fellow! He was afraid not even Miss Woodhouse' – he stopt a moment – 'or Miss Smith could inspire him.'

The very next day however produced some proof of inspiration. He called for a few moments, just to leave a piece of paper on the table containing, as he said, a charade, which a friend of his had addressed to a young lady, the object of his admiration, but which, from his manner, Emma was immediately convinced must be his own.

'I do not offer it for Miss Smith's collection,' said he. 'Being my friend's, I have no right to expose it in any degree to the public eye, but perhaps you may not dislike looking at it.'

The speech was more to Emma than to Harriet, which Emma could understand. There was deep consciousness about him, and he found it easier to meet her eye than her friend's. He was gone the next moment: – after another moment's pause,

'Take it,' said Emma, smiling, and pushing the paper towards Harriet – 'it is for you. Take your own.'

Volume 1, Chapter 10

Emma tells Harriet that she has none of the 'usual inducements' to marry, that is to say, she already has social position and economic security. Harriet draws a shrewd comparison between Emma and the spinster Miss Bates, which Emma rejects outright: 'between *us* there never can be any likeness, except in being unmarried'. Emma is shown to be in error with her comments about spinsters: 'A single woman, with a very narrow income, must be a ridiculous, disagreeable, old maid', for, as she admits, this is not the case with Miss Bates, who is generally beloved. Emma's description of the deleterious effect of poverty on character, 'a very narrow income has a tendency to contract the mind, and sour the temper', is ironically a more fitting description of Mrs Churchill, who has wealth and status (see Contemporary Documents, **p. 23**).

'I have none of the usual inducements of women to marry. Were I to fall in love, indeed, it would be a different thing! but I never have been in love; it is not my way, or my nature; and I do not think I ever shall. And, without love, I am sure I should be a fool to change such a situation as mine. Fortune I do not want; employment I do not want; consequence I do not want: I believe few married women are half as much mistress of their husband's house, as I am of Hartfield; and never, never could I expect to be so truly beloved and important; so always first and always right in any man's eyes as I am in my father's.'

'But then, to be an old maid at last, like Miss Bates!'

'That is as formidable an image as you could present, Harriet; and if I thought I should ever be like Miss Bates! so silly – so satisfied – so smiling – so prosing – so undistinguishing and unfastidious – and so apt to tell every thing relative to every body about me, I would marry to-morrow. But between *us*, I am convinced there never can be any likeness, except in being unmarried.'

'But still, you will be an old maid! and that's so dreadful!'

'Never mind, Harriet, I shall not be a poor old maid; and it is poverty only which makes celibacy contemptible to a generous public! A single woman, with a very narrow income, must be a ridiculous, disagreeable, old maid! the proper sport of boys and girls; but a single woman, of good fortune, is always respectable, and may be as sensible and pleasant as anybody else. And the distinction is not quite so much against the candour and common sense of the world as appears at first; for a very narrow income has a tendency to contract the mind, and sour the temper. Those who can barely live, and who live perforce in a very small, and generally very inferior, society, may well be illiberal and cross. This does not apply, however, to Miss Bates; she is only too good natured and too silly to suit me; but, in general, she is very much to the taste of everybody, though single and though poor. Poverty certainly has not contracted her mind: I really believe, if she had only a shilling in the world, she would be very likely to give away sixpence of it; and nobody is afraid of her: that is a great charm.'

Emma's visit to the poor has caused much controversy amongst critics, some of whom have taken umbrage at Austen's depiction of the lower classes (see **pp. 73–4**). Others have viewed this passage as a pertinent example of Austen's caustic irony, arguing that although Emma claims to be affected by the distressing scene, she very quickly forgets all about it when she sees Mr Elton. However, a careful reading of the passage shows Emma to be kind and compassionate: she does not quickly pass over the poor. Even when she meets Mr Elton, they discuss 'what could and should be done'. Furthermore, Emma's intelligent response to the distressing scene shines through. She does not patronize 'the poor' by merely feeling sorry for them, nor does she have any romantic illusions about them; she does what she can but leaves them with their dignity: 'If we feel for the wretched, enough to do all we can for them, the rest is empty sympathy, only distressing to ourselves'. Austen here provides a contrast to the idealization of the poor in the sentimental novel.

They were now approaching the cottage, and all idle topics were superseded. Emma was very compassionate; and the distresses of the poor were as sure of relief from her personal attention and kindness, her counsel and her patience, as from her purse. She understood their ways, could allow for their ignorance and their temptations, had no romantic expectations of extraordinary virtue from those, for whom education had done so little; entered into their troubles with ready sympathy, and always gave her assistance with as much intelligence as good-will. In the present instance, it was sickness and poverty together which she came to visit; and after remaining there as long as she could give comfort or advice, she quitted the cottage with such an impression of the scene as made her say to Harriet, as they walked away,

'These are the sights, Harriet, to do one good. How trifling they make every thing else appear! – I feel now as if I could think of nothing but these poor creatures all the rest of the day; and yet, who can say how soon it may all vanish from my mind?'

'Very true,' said Harriet. 'Poor creatures! one can think of nothing else.'

'And really, I do not think the impression will soon be over,' said Emma, as she crossed the low hedge, and tottering footstep which ended the narrow, slippery path through the cottage garden, and brought them into the lane again. 'I do not think it will,' stopping to look once more at all the outward wretchedness of the place, and recal [*sic*] the still greater within.

'Oh! dear, no,' said her companion.

They walked on. The lane made a slight bend; and when that bend was passed, Mr Elton was immediately in sight; and so near as to give Emma time only to say farther,

'Ah! Harriet, here comes a very sudden trial of our stability in good thoughts. Well, (smiling,) I hope it may be allowed that if compassion has produced exertion and relief to the sufferers, it has done all that is truly important. If we feel for the wretched, enough to do all we can for them, the rest is empty sympathy, only distressing to ourselves.

Volume I, Chapter 12

Emma is reconciled with Mr Knightley, who is unable to resist (as Emma is all too aware) the baby girl dancing in her aunt's arms (see Contemporary Documents, **p. 25**). Austen describes the 'true English style' of George and John Knightley's speech. Knightley is portrayed as a progressive farmer, as revealed by his endorsement of the new technique of crop-rotation. Furthermore, his responsibilities to the land and to the rights of the villagers are shown in his refusal to engage in act of enclosure (see **pp. 91–2, 117–18**).

Throughout *Emma*, Austen explores the importance of verbal ambiguities, equivocations, comic misunderstandings, riddles and word-games. Frank Churchill is the prime exemplar of verbal charm and manipulation. In contrast, the Knightley brothers are associated with a lack of gallantry and a love of plain-speaking, which Austen describes as the 'true English style'. 'Real attachment' belies the gruff exterior of the language between the brothers. The association of a certain kind of brusqueness and forthrightness with genuine feeling is used repeatedly in *Emma* to encapsulate the very essence of Englishness (see **pp. 91, 117**).

She hoped they might now become friends again. She thought it was time to make up. Making-up indeed would not do. *She* certainly had not been in the wrong, and *he* would never own that he had. Concession must be out of the question; but it was time to appear to forget that they had ever quarrelled; and she hoped it might rather assist the restoration of friendship, that when he came into the room she had one of the children with her – the youngest, a nice little girl about eight months old, who was now making her first visit to Hartfield, and very happy to be danced about in her aunt's arms. It did assist; for though he began with grave looks and short questions, he was soon led on to talk of them all in the usual way, and to take the child out of her arms with all the unceremoniousness of perfect amity. [. . .]

This had just taken place and with great cordiality, when John Knightley made his appearance, and 'How d'ye do, George?' and 'John, how are you?' succeeded in the true English style, burying under a calmness that seemed all but indifference, the real attachment which would have led either of them, if requisite, to do every thing for the good of the other. [. . .] The plan of a drain, the change of a fence, the felling of a tree, and the destination of every acre for wheat, turnips, or spring corn, was entered into with as much equality of interest by John, as his cooler manners rendered possible.

'[. . .] But John, as to what I was telling you of my idea of moving the path to Langham, of turning it more to the right that it may not cut through the home meadows, I cannot conceive any difficulty. I should not attempt it, if it were to be the means of inconvenience to the Highbury people'.

Volume 1, Chapter 15

The Christmas Eve party at Randalls has ended, and Emma finds herself alone in the carriage with Mr Elton. She has dismissed John Knightley's warning that she is the object of Elton's interest, and is shocked by his sudden proposal of marriage.

Austen's comedy of errors between Emma, Elton and Harriet reaches its climax. Austen draws much comedy from the scene: it is very rare for a man and woman to be left alone, and Elton has only minutes to make his proposal. Furthermore, he misunderstands Emma's initial stunned silence for a sign of encouragement, only to be rejected outright:

> 'Charming Miss Woodhouse! allow me to interpret this interesting silence. It confesses that you have long understood me.'
> 'No, sir,' cried Emma, 'it confesses no such thing'.

The misunderstandings are unravelled, and the comic irony increased as Elton insists that Emma has given him 'encouragement'. The high comedy of Mr Elton's proposal is enhanced by Emma's unwitting compliance in the mistake. Emma's incredulity at finding herself the object of Mr Elton's desire is paralleled with his disdain at the discovery that the illegitimate Harriet is intended for himself: 'I think seriously of Miss Smith! . . . no doubt, there are men who might not object to – Every body has their level: but as for myself, I am not, I think, quite so much at a loss.'

'Good heaven!' cried Mr Elton, 'what can be the meaning of this? – Miss Smith! – I never thought of Miss Smith in the whole course of my existence – never paid her any attentions, but as your friend: never cared whether she were dead or alive, but as your friend. If she has fancied otherwise, her own wishes have misled her, and I am very sorry – extremely sorry – But, Miss Smith, indeed! – Oh! Miss Woodhouse! who can think of Miss Smith, when Miss Woodhouse is near! No, upon my honour, there is no unsteadiness of character. I have thought only of you. I protest against having paid the smallest attention to any one else. Every thing that I have said or done, for many weeks past, has been with the sole view of marking my adoration of yourself. You cannot really, seriously, doubt it. No! – (in an accent meant to be insinuating) – I am sure you have seen and understood me.'

It would be impossible to say what Emma felt, on hearing this – which of all her unpleasant sensations was uppermost. She was too completely overpowered to be immediately able to reply: and two moments of silence being ample encourage-ment for Mr Elton's sanguine state of mind, he tried to take her hand again, as he joyously exclaimed –

'Charming Miss Woodhouse! allow me to interpret this interesting silence. It confesses that you have long understood me.'

'No, sir,' cried Emma, 'it confesses no such thing. So far from having long understood you, I have been in a most complete error with respect to your views, till this moment. As to myself, I am very sorry that you should have been giving way to any feelings – Nothing could be farther from my wishes – your attachment to my friend Harriet – your pursuit of her, (pursuit, it appeared,) gave me great pleasure, and I have been very earnestly wishing you success: but had I supposed that she were not your attraction to Hartfield, I should certainly have thought you judged ill in making your visits so frequent. Am I to believe that you have never sought to recommend yourself particularly to Miss Smith? – that you have never thought seriously of her?'

'Never, madam,' cried he, affronted, in his turn: 'never, I assure you. I think seriously of Miss Smith! – Miss Smith is a very good sort of girl; and I should be happy to see her respectably settled. I wish her extremely well: and, no doubt, there are men who might not object to – Every body has their level: but as for myself, I am not, I think, quite so much at a loss. I need not so totally despair of an equal alliance, as to be addressing myself to Miss Smith! – No, madam, my visits to Hartfield have been for yourself only; and the encouragement I received' –

'Encouragement! – I give you encouragement! – sir, you have been entirely mistaken in supposing it. I have seen you only as the admirer of my friend. In no other light could you have been more to me than a common acquaintance. I am exceedingly sorry: but it is well that the mistake ends where it does. Had the same behaviour continued, Miss Smith might have been led into a misconception of your views; not being aware, probably, any more than myself, of the very great inequality which you are so sensible of. But, as it is, the disappointment is single, and, I trust, will not be lasting. I have no thoughts of matrimony at present.'

Volume 1, Chapter 16

In contrast to the dramatic quality of the carriage scene, the first half of the next chapter provides an insight into Emma's private thoughts, as she reflects upon her mistakes. Emma is genuinely concerned about the prospect of Harriet's unhappiness, and she recognizes that she has been in error in her stubborn refusal to see the truth and her manipulation of Harriet. She also sees that she has fabricated the romance 'and made everything bend to it'. Her ruminations on Mr Elton lead her to realize that 'though sighs and fine words had been given in abundance ... there had been no real affection either in his language or manners'. Furthermore, she understands that he is a social climber who 'only wanted to aggrandize and enrich himself'. The great comic paradox is that Emma is angry with Elton for looking down on Harriet, but is equally furious that he looks up to her level: 'so well understanding the gradations of rank below him, and be so blind to what rose above'. Having shown the worst effects of social snobbery in Mr Elton's dismissal of Harriet, the authorial irony re-establishes its attack on Emma, whose own snobbishness has yet to be purged: 'He must know that the Woodhouses had been settled for several generations at Hartfield, the younger branch of a very ancient family – and that the Eltons were nobody.'

The comic misunderstandings within the Emma/Harriet/Elton love triangle are made possible by their tenuous grasp of social realities in relation to rank and station. Harriet believes (or is made to believe) that she is worthy of Mr Elton, whilst he, in turn, believes that he is worthy of Emma. Emma's concurrence in the misunderstandings is in no small part due to the fact that she is unable to conceive that Mr Elton could aspire to her own lofty level.

Nevertheless, Emma's endearing honesty forces her to admit that she has unwittingly encouraged his suit: 'If *she* had so mis-interpreted his feelings, she had little right to wonder that *he*, with self-interest to blind him, should have mistaken her's.' Emma resolves not to match-make again, but her relapse at the end of the passage suggests otherwise.

The hair was curled, and the maid sent away, and Emma sat down to think and be miserable. – It was a wretched business, indeed! – Such an overthrow of every thing she had been wishing for! – Such a development of every thing most unwelcome! – Such a blow for Harriet! – That was the worst of all. Every part of it brought pain and humiliation, of some sort or other; but, compared with the evil to Harriet, all was light; and she would gladly have submitted to feel yet more mistaken – more in error – more disgraced by mis-judgment, than she actually was, could the effects of her blunders have been confined to herself.

'If I had not persuaded Harriet into liking the man, I could have borne any thing. He might have doubled his presumption to me – But poor Harriet!'

How she could have been so deceived! – He protested that he had never thought seriously of Harriet – never! She looked back as well as she could; but it was all confusion. She had taken up the idea, she supposed, and made every thing bend to it. His manners, however, must have been unmarked, wavering, dubious, or she could not have been so misled.

The picture! – How eager he had been about the picture! – and the charade! – and an hundred other circumstances; – how clearly they had seemed to point at Harriet. [. . .]

She thought nothing of his attachment, and was insulted by his hopes. He wanted to marry well, and having the arrogance to raise his eyes to her, pretended to be in love; but she was perfectly easy as to his not suffering any disappointment that need be cared for. There had been no real affection either in his language or manners. Sighs and fine words had been given in abundance; but she could hardly devise any set of expressions, or fancy any tone of voice, less allied with real love . . . he only wanted to aggrandize and enrich himself; and if Miss Woodhouse of Hartfield, the heiress of thirty thousand pounds[1] were not quite so easily obtained as he had fancied, he would soon try for Miss Somebody else with twenty, or with ten.

But – that he should talk of encouragement, should consider her as aware of his views, accepting his attentions, meaning (in short), to marry him! – should suppose himself her equal in connection or mind! – look down upon her friend, so well understanding the gradations of rank below him, and be so blind to what rose above, as to fancy himself shewing no presumption in addressing her! – It was most provoking.

Perhaps it was not fair to expect him to feel how very much he was her inferior in talent, and all the elegancies of mind. The very want of such equality might prevent his perception of it; but he must know that in fortune and consequence she was greatly his superior. He must know that the Woodhouses had been settled for several generations at Hartfield, the younger branch of a very ancient family – and that the Eltons were nobody. The landed property of Hartfield certainly was inconsiderable, being but a sort of notch in the Donwell Abbey estate, to which all the rest of Highbury belonged; but their fortune, from other sources, was such as to make them scarcely secondary to Donwell Abbey itself, in every other kind of consequence; and the Woodhouses had long held a high place in the consideration of the neighbourhood which Mr Elton had first entered not two years ago, to make his way as he could, without any alliances but in trade, or any thing to recommend him to notice but his situation and his civility. – But he had fancied her in love with him; that evidently must have been his dependence; and after raving a little about the seeming incongruity of gentle manners and a conceited head, Emma was obliged in common honesty to stop and admit that her own behaviour to him had been so complaisant and obliging, so full of courtesy and attention, as (supposing her real motive unperceived) might warrant a man of ordinary observation and delicacy, like Mr Elton, in fancying himself a very decided favourite. If *she* had so mis-interpreted his feelings, she had little right to wonder that *he*, with self-interest to blind him, should have mistaken her's.

The first error and the worst lay at her door. It was foolish, it was wrong to take so active a part in bringing two people together. It was adventuring too far, assuming too much, making light of what ought to be serious, a trick of what ought to be simple. She was quite concerned and ashamed, and resolved to do such things no more.

– I have been but half a friend to her; and if she were *not* to feel this disappointment so very much, I am sure I have not an idea of any body else who would be at all desirable for her; – William Cox – Oh! No, I could not endure William Cox – a pert young lawyer.'

She stopt to blush and laugh at her own relapse, and then resumed a more serious, more dispiriting cogitation upon what had been, and might be, and must be.

---

1   £1.2 million by today's standards.

Volume 1, Chapter 18

It is unsurprising that Mr Knightley, the advocate of forthrightness and 'frankness', should take a dislike to Frank, although jealousy distorts his judgement. It is Frank's language, expressed in a fine flourishing letter, full of professions and falsehoods, which enables Mr Knightley to clarify the indefinable 'something' that had eluded him in his early analysis of right moral conduct. 'No, Emma, your amiable young man can be amiable only in French, not in English.' English plainness is contrasted with French affectation and gallantry. The contrast of Mr Knightley's bluntness with Frank's charm, associated with dangerous French individualism, has encouraged some critics to view Mr Knightley as an exemplar of English patriotism (see **pp. 91–2**). Frank's character is revealed in his 'fine flourishing letter' as Robert Martin's 'genuine delicacy' is revealed in his letter. Emma reads both characters wrongly.

'We shall never agree about him,' cried Emma; 'but that is nothing extraordinary. I have not the least idea of his being a weak young man: I feel sure that he is not. Mr Weston would not be blind to folly, though in his own son; but he is very likely to have a more yielding, complying, mild disposition than would suit your notions of man's perfection. I dare say he has; and though it may cut him off from some advantages, it will secure him many others.'

'Yes; all the advantages of sitting still when he ought to move, and of leading a life of mere idle pleasure, and fancying himself extremely expert in finding excuses for it. He can sit down and write a fine flourishing letter, full of professions and falsehoods, and persuade himself that he has hit upon the very best method in the world of preserving peace at home and preventing his father's having any right to complain. His letters disgust me.'

'Your feelings are singular. They seem to satisfy every body else.'

'I suspect they do not satisfy Mrs Weston. They hardly can satisfy a woman of her good sense and quick feelings: standing in a mother's place, but without a mother's affection to blind her. It is on her account that attention to Randalls is doubly due, and she must doubly feel the omission. Had she been a person of consequence herself, he would have come I dare say; and it would not have signified whether he did or no. Can you think your friend behind-hand in these sort of considerations? Do you suppose she does not often say all this to herself? No, Emma, your amiable young man can be amiable only in French, not in English. He may be very "aimable," have very good manners, and be very agreeable; but he can have no English delicacy towards the feelings of other people: nothing really amiable about him.'

'You seem determined to think ill of him.'

'Me! – not at all,' replied Mr Knightley, rather displeased; 'I do not want to think ill of him. I should be as ready to acknowledge his merits as any other man; but I hear of none, except what are merely personal; that he is well grown and good-looking, with smooth, plausible manners.'

Volume 2, Chapter 7

In the second of the novel's three volumes, the Jane Fairfax/Frank Churchill plot becomes prominent, and Mr Elton merges into the background, with his new bride occupying a more central place. Emma, with the complicity of Frank Churchill, concocts a fantasy about a secret love affair between Jane Fairfax and her friend's husband, Mr Dixon.

The Coles are an example of an upwardly mobile family, who have risen through trade to a place of prominence in the village of Highbury.

Here Austen ironizes her heroine through the use of free indirect speech. Despite her desire to attend the party, Emma decides that she will refuse her invitation: 'Nothing should tempt *her* to go . . . The Coles were very respectable in their way, but they ought to be taught that it was not for them to arrange the terms on which the superior families would visit them.' There is a neat irony in the fact that Emma considers an invitation to the Coles' party as an 'insult' and a presumption unworthy of their rank and station, yet she is mortified when she discovers that no such 'insult' has arrived. Emma is representing an archetypal snobbish position towards new money or the *nouveaux riches*. However, Emma's attitude evolves and changes. The Coles, as Emma places them, are 'of low origin, in trade, and only moderately genteel', yet she learns to accept the Cole family into genteel Highbury because they show 'real attention', unlike Mrs Elton, who also represents new money, but is vulgar and selfish (see **pp. 80–1**). The second paragraph shows, in D. W. Harding's phrase, Austen's 'regulated hatred' and her frustration at the limits of her own society: 'nothing worse than every day remarks, dull repetitions, old news, and heavy jokes' (see **pp. 53–4**).

This was the occurrence: – The Coles had been settled some years in Highbury, and were very good sort of people – friendly, liberal, and unpretending; but, on the other hand, they were of low origin, in trade, and only moderately genteel. On their first coming into the country, they had lived in proportion to their income, quietly, keeping little company, and that little unexpensively; but the last year or two had brought them a considerable increase of means – the house in town had yielded greater profits, and fortune in general had smiled on them. With their wealth, their views increased; their want of a larger house, their inclination for more company. They added to their house, to their number of servants, to their expenses of every sort; and by this time were, in fortune and style of living, second only to the family at Hartfield. Their love of society, and their new dining-room, prepared every body for their keeping dinner-company; and a few parties, chiefly among the single men, had already taken place. The regular and best families Emma could hardly suppose they would presume to invite – neither Donwell, nor Hartfield, nor Randalls. Nothing should tempt *her* to go, if they did; and she regretted that her father's known habits would be giving her refusal less meaning than she could wish. The Coles were very respectable in their way, but they ought to be taught that it was not for them to arrange the terms on which the superior families would visit them. This lesson, she very much feared, they would receive only from herself; she had little hope of Mr Knightley, none of Mr Weston.

But she had made up her mind how to meet this presumption so many weeks before it appeared, that when the insult came at last, it found her very differently affected. Donwell and Randalls had received their invitation, and none had come for her father and herself; and Mrs Weston's accounting for it with 'I suppose they will not take the liberty with you; they know you do not dine out,' was not quite sufficient. She felt that she should like to have had the power of refusal; and afterwards, as the idea of the party to be assembled there, consisting precisely of those whose society was dearest to her, occurred again and again, she did not know that she might not have been tempted to accept. Harriet was to be there in the evening, and the Bateses. They had been speaking of it as they walked about Highbury the day before, and Frank Churchill had most earnestly lamented her absence. Might not the evening end in a dance? had been a question of his. The bare possibility of it acted as a further irritation on her spirits; and her being left in solitary grandeur, even supposing the omission to be intended as a compliment, was but poor comfort. [. . .]

[. . .] the rest of the dinner [at the Coles] passed away; the dessert succeeded, the children came in, and were talked to and admired amid the usual rate of conversation; a few clever things said, a few downright silly, but by much the larger proportion neither the one nor the other – nothing worse than every day remarks, dull repetitions, old news, and heavy jokes.

Volume 2, Chapter 9

This vivid description of everyday life in Highbury would appear to contradict the apparent rigidity of the class structure in *Emma* (see **pp. 57, 73–5**). Here, we see Highbury as a thriving, busy community of butcher and baker, with children and dogs playing in the street. The descriptive sequence – quite unusual in Jane Austen, though re-used to brilliant emotional effect as the background to the love-climax of her last completed novel, *Persuasion* – also shows how boredom spurs Emma's imagination, and not, this time, in a negative sense. She has the capacity to find pleasure and interest in what others might consider banal. This passage traces the movement of Emma's mind, as she uses her imagination to amuse herself and make things interesting to herself. The passage is also ironic, as it shows the discrepancy between what Emma expects to find (Mr Perry, William Cox, etc.), and what she does find.

Harriet, tempted by every thing and swayed by half a word, was always very long at a purchase; and while she was still hanging over muslins and changing her mind, Emma went to the door for amusement. – Much could not be hoped from the traffic of even the busiest part of Highbury; – Mr Perry walking hastily by, Mr William Cox letting himself in at the office door, Mr Cole's carriage horses returning from exercise, or a stray letter-boy on an obstinate mule, were the liveliest objects she could presume to expect; and when her eyes fell only on the butcher with his tray, a tidy old woman travelling homewards from shop with her full basket, two curs quarrelling over a dirty bone, and a string of dawdling children round the baker's little bow-window eyeing the gingerbread, she knew she had no reason to complain, and was amused enough; quite enough still to stand at the door. A mind lively and at ease, can do with seeing nothing, and can see nothing that does not answer.

Volume 2, Chapter 10

One of the effects of the narrative being so closely tied to Emma's thought processes is that we often make the same mistakes as her. The reader is not allowed a glimpse of Frank's unspoken thoughts or inner life, as this would give away the game completely. The reader shares Emma's puzzlement; our incomplete understanding of the text parallels her imperfect comprehension of the scene she is witnessing. Frank's mastery of word-play is shown in this scene. This is at its most skilful and scintillating when he is able to play Emma and Jane off against each other. Frank flexes his verbal muscles by playing a flirtatious double game. He uses the opportunity to make love to Jane, whilst simultaneously continuing the Dixon pretence with Emma and using her as a blind. Thus, he speaks of the pianoforte as a gift 'thoroughly from the heart'. Emma, thinking he alludes to Dixon, is quick to reprimand Frank's indiscretion – 'you speak too plain' – but he replies with insouciance, 'I would have her understand me. I am not in the least ashamed of my meaning.'

'Whoever Col. Campbell might employ,' said Frank Churchill, with a smile at Emma, 'the person has not chosen ill. I heard a good deal of Col. Campbell's taste at Weymouth; and the softness of the upper notes I am sure is exactly what he and *all that party* would particularly prize. I dare say, Miss Fairfax, that he either gave his friend very minute directions, or wrote to Broadwood himself. Do not you think so?'

Jane did not look round. She was not obliged to hear. Mrs Weston had been speaking to her at the same moment.

'It is not fair,' said Emma in a whisper, 'mine was a random guess. Do not distress her.'

He shook his head with a smile, and looked as if he had very little doubt and very little mercy. Soon afterwards he began again,

'How much your friends in Ireland must be enjoying your pleasure on this occasion, Miss Fairfax'. . . . I have the pleasure Madam, (to Mrs Bates,) of restoring your spectacles, healed for the present.'

He was very warmly thanked both by mother and daughter; to escape a little from the latter, he went to the pianoforte, and begged Miss Fairfax, who was still sitting at it, to play something more.

'If you are very kind,' said he, 'it will be one of the waltzes we danced last night; – let me live them over again. You did not enjoy them as I did; you appeared tired the whole time. I believe you were glad we danced no longer; but I would have given worlds – all the worlds one ever has to give – for another half hour.'

She played.

'What felicity it is to hear a tune again which *has* made one happy! –If I mistake not that was danced at Weymouth.'

She looked up at him for a moment, coloured deeply, and played something else. He took some music from a chair near the pianoforte, and turning to Emma, said,

'Here is something quite new to me. Do you know it? – Cramer. – And here are a new set of Irish melodies. That, from such a quarter, one might expect. This was all sent with the instrument. Very thoughtful of Col. Campbell, was not it? – He knew Miss Fairfax could have no music here. I honour that part of the attention particularly; it shews it to have been so thoroughly from the heart. Nothing hastily done; nothing incomplete. True affection only could have prompted it.'

Emma wished he would be less pointed, yet could not help being amused; and when on glancing her eye towards Jane Fairfax she caught the remains of a smile, when she saw that with all the deep blush of consciousness, there had been a smile of secret delight, she had less scruple in the amusement, and much less compunction with respect to her. – This amiable, upright, perfect Jane Fairfax was apparently cherishing very reprehensible feelings.

Volume 2, Chapter 12

> Frank is on the brink of making a confession of love. The reader is able to pick up on the hints that are given (he has just been to visit Jane Fairfax) and so to realize that the object of his affection is Jane rather than Emma. Emma's misinterpretation of Frank's feelings is yet another example of Austen's comic irony, whereby the reader recognizes an alternative version of reality than Emma's: 'He was more in love with her than Emma had supposed'. Austen parallels Emma's delusion here with her earlier delusion concerning Mr Elton, although this time Emma's own feelings are directly engaged. She imagines herself to be 'a little in love with Frank Churchill'.

'As you do us such ample justice now,' said Emma, laughing, 'I will venture to ask, whether you did not come a little doubtingly at first? Do not we rather surpass your expectations? I am sure we do. I am sure you did not much expect to like us. You would not have been so long in coming, if you had had a pleasant idea of Highbury.'

He laughed rather consciously; and though denying the sentiment, Emma was convinced that it had been so.

'And you must be off this very morning?'

'Yes; my father is to join me here: we shall walk back together, and I must be off immediately. I am almost afraid that every moment will bring him.'

'Not five minutes to spare even for your friends Miss Fairfax and Miss Bates? How unlucky! Miss Bates's powerful, argumentative mind might have strengthened yours.'

'Yes – I *have* called there; passing the door, I thought it better. It was a right thing to do. I went in for three minutes, and was detained by Miss Bates's being absent. She was out; and I felt it impossible not to wait till she came in. She is a woman that one may, that one *must* laugh at; but that one would not wish to slight. It was better to pay my visit, then' –

He hesitated, got up, walked to a window.

'In short,' said he, 'perhaps, Miss Woodhouse – I think you can hardly be quite without suspicion' –

He looked at her, as if wanting to read her thoughts. She hardly knew what to say. It seemed like the forerunner of something absolutely serious, which she did not wish. Forcing herself to speak, therefore, in the hope of putting it by, she calmly said,

'You were quite in the right; it was most natural to pay your visit, then' –

He was silent. She believed he was looking at her; probably reflecting on what she had said, and trying to understand the manner. She heard him sigh. It was natural for him to feel that he had *cause* to sigh. He could not believe her to be encouraging him. A few awkward moments passed, and he sat down again; and in a more determined manner said,

'It was something to feel that all the rest of my time might be given to Hartfield. My regard for Hartfield is most warm' –

He stopt again, rose again, and seemed quite embarrassed. – He was more in love with her than Emma had supposed; and who can say how it might have ended, if his father had not made his appearance? [. . .]

It was a sad change. They had been meeting almost every day since his arrival. Certainly his being at Randalls had given great spirit to the last two weeks – indescribable spirit; the idea, the expectation of seeing him which every morning had brought, the assurance of his attentions, his liveliness, his manners! It had been a very happy fortnight, and forlorn must be the sinking from it into the common course of Hartfield days. To complete every other recommendation, he had *almost* told her that he loved her. What strength, or what constancy of affection he might be subject to, was another point; but at present she could not doubt his having a decidedly warm admiration, a conscious preference of herself; and this persuasion, joined to all the rest, made her think that she *must* be a little in love with him, in spite of every previous determination against it.

Volume 2, Chapter 17

In Frank's absence the others discuss Jane's future as a governess. Jane has been discovered walking to the post office in the rain and Emma presumes that she is writing to Mr Dixon. Mrs Elton continues to patronize Jane Fairfax.

Mrs Elton is the source of much comedy and social satire, aimed at upstart members of the commercial middle classes, who have money but lack social refinement. With her airs and pretensions, she confirms Emma's worst prejudices about 'trade'. Mrs Elton's speech is peppered with slang and modish phrases, and she is occasionally ungrammatical. She is one of Austen's most wonderfully grotesque comic creations, with her incessant boasting of the rich Sucklings of Maple Grove – note the pun contained in the name when she boasts of the 'Bragge' family. Her idiosyncratic speech captures her own particular brand of vulgarity: 'every body was anxious to be in her family, for she moves in the first circle. Wax-candles in the school-room! You may imagine how desirable!'

Mrs Elton also uses her position of 'Lady Patroness' to bully Jane Fairfax and humiliate Harriet Smith, both of them vulnerable, poor, single women. There is some sharp social satire on the fate of penniless unmarried women, which is compared to the slave-trade, 'Offices for the sale – not quite of human flesh – but of human intellect.' Jane refers to the employment agencies for governesses, a fate from which she makes a very narrow escape. Becoming a governess is one of the only professions available to educated women. But she is well aware that looking after Mrs Smallridge's three children for a pittance is a life of drudgery with very little social status. The usual option for well-bred, beautiful and educated women such as Jane Fairfax is to make a 'good' marriage: her union with Frank Churchill frees her from a life of 'slavery'.

'I not aware!' said Jane, shaking her head; 'dear Mrs Elton, who can have thought of it as I have done?'

'But you have not seen so much of the world as I have. You do not know how many candidates there always are for the *first* situations. I saw a vast deal of that in the neighbourhood round Maple Grove. A cousin of Mr Suckling, Mrs Bragge, had such an infinity of applications; every body was anxious to be in her family, for she moves in the first circle. Wax-candles in the school-room! You may imagine how desirable! Of all houses in the kingdom Mrs Bragge's is the one I would most wish to see you in.'

'Col. and Mrs Campbell are to be in town again by midsummer,' said Jane. 'I must spend some time with them; I am sure they will want it; – afterwards I may probably be glad to dispose of myself. But I would not wish you to take the trouble of making any inquiries at present.'

'Trouble! aye, I know your scruples. You are afraid of giving me trouble; but I assure you, my dear Jane, the Campbells can hardly be more interested about you than I am. I shall write to Mrs Partridge in a day or two, and shall give her a strict charge to be on the look-out for any thing eligible.'

'Thank you, but I would rather you did not mention the subject to her; till the time draws nearer, I do not wish to be giving any body trouble.'

'But, my dear child, the time *is* drawing near; here is April, and June, or say even July, is very near, with such business to accomplish before us. Your inexperience really amuses me! A situation such as you deserve, and your friends would require for you, is no every day occurrence, is not obtained at a moment's notice; indeed, indeed, we must begin inquiring directly.'

'Excuse me, ma'am, but this is by no means my intention; I make no inquiry myself, and should be sorry to have any made by my friends. When I am quite determined as to the time, I am not at all afraid of being long unemployed. There are places in town, offices, where inquiry would soon produce something – Offices for the sale – not quite of human flesh – but of human intellect.'

'Oh! my dear, human flesh! You quite shock me; if you mean a fling at the slave-trade, I assure you Mr Suckling was always rather a friend to the abolition.'[1]

'I did not mean, I was not thinking of the slave-trade,' replied Jane; 'governess-trade, I assure you, was all that I had in view; widely different certainly as to the guilt of those who carry it on; but as to the greater misery of the victims, I do not know where it lies. But I only mean to say that there are advertising offices, and that by applying to them I should have no doubt of very soon meeting with something that would do.'

Volume 3, Chapter 2

Mr Elton snubs Harriet at the Crown Ball by refusing to dance with her, but she is rescued from her social humiliation by Mr Knightley.

In *Emma*, Austen shows how language is vulnerable to evasions and misconstructions, but offsets this by demonstrating the unmistakable power of non-verbal communication. The most memorable moments are often expressed by wordless actions, such as when Mr Knightley almost kisses Emma's hand. Very often, strong feeling is rendered by the frequency with which couples look at each other. Mr Knightley rumbles Jane and Frank long before anyone else because he notices the way they look at each other. In *Emma*, Austen explores the impact of a particular kind of telepathy between couples. When Harriet is snubbed by Mr Elton at the Crown Ball, it is made clear that Mrs Elton is complicit: 'smiles of high glee passed between him and his wife'. But when Harriet is saved by Mr Knightley, we witness the loving telepathy between him and Emma: 'her eyes invited him irresistibly to come to her and be thanked.'

---

1   Mrs Elton comes from the slave-port of Bristol. The slave-trade was abolished, after fierce debate, in 1807–8. Jane Austen greatly admired the abolitionist Thomas Clarkson. Postcolonial critics have made much of the fact that Sir Thomas Bertram in *Mansfield Park* has sugar-plantations in Antigua, so is therefore a slave-owner.

In public, their dialogue is distinguished by an economy of expression, which contrasts refreshingly with the tortuous, circuitous way in which, for example, Jane and Frank are forced to communicate in public. Emma and Knightley's romantic involvement is characterized by an absence of sentimental language and false courtesy:

> 'Whom are you going to dance with?' asked Mr Knightley.
> She hesitated a moment, and then replied, 'With you, if you will ask me.'
> 'Will you?' said he, offering his hand.
> 'Indeed I will.'

The declaration that they need not regard themselves as brother and sister is also important in setting up the romantic ending.

Emma had no opportunity of speaking to Mr Knightley till after supper; but, when they were all in the ball-room again, her eyes invited him irresistibly to come to her and be thanked. He was warm in his reprobation of Mr Elton's conduct; it had been unpardonable rudeness; and Mrs Elton's looks also received the due share of censure.

'They aimed at wounding more than Harriet,' said he. 'Emma, why is it that they are your enemies?'

He looked with smiling penetration; and, on receiving no answer, added, '*She* ought not to be angry with you, I suspect, whatever he may be. – To that surmise, you say nothing, of course; but confess, Emma, that you did want him to marry Harriet.'

'I did,' replied Emma, 'and they cannot forgive me.'

He shook his head; but there was a smile of indulgence with it, and he only said, 'I shall not scold you. I leave you to your own reflections.'

'Can you trust me with such flatterers? – Does my vain spirit ever tell me I am wrong?'

'Not your vain spirit, but your serious spirit. – If one leads you wrong, I am sure the other tells you of it.'

'I do own myself to have been completely mistaken in Mr Elton. There is a littleness about him which you discovered, and which I did not: and I was fully convinced of his being in love with Harriet. It was through a series of strange blunders!'

'And, in return for your acknowledging so much, I will do you the justice to say, that you would have chosen for him better than he has chosen for himself. – Harriet Smith has some first-rate qualities, which Mrs Elton is totally without. An unpretending, single-minded, artless girl – infinitely to be preferred by any man of sense and taste to such a woman as Mrs Elton. I found Harriet more conversable than I expected.'

Emma was extremely gratified. – They were interrupted by the bustle of Mr Weston calling on every body to begin dancing again.

'Come Miss Woodhouse, Miss Otway, Miss Fairfax, what are you all doing? – Come Emma, set your companions the example. Every body is lazy! Every body is asleep!'

'I am ready,' said Emma, 'whenever I am wanted.'

'Whom are you going to dance with?' asked Mr Knightley.

She hesitated a moment, and then replied, 'With you, if you will ask me.'

'Will you?' said he, offering his hand.

'Indeed I will. You have shown that you can dance, and you know we are not really so much brother and sister as to make it at all improper.'

'Brother and sister! no, indeed.'

Volume 3, Chapter 3

Harriet arrives at Hartfield in a distressed state, supported by Frank Churchill, who has rescued her from a party of gypsies. Harriet's adventure and her rescue by a gallant gentleman, once again arouse Emma's romantic imagination.

Harriet and Miss Bickerton's encounter with the gypsies has incited commentary from Marxist critics, who have viewed it as an example of Austen's class-bound anxieties with regard to the lower orders (see p. 75). For such critics, the gypsies are 'a perfect symbol for the masses of uprooted people who were dispossessed, landless, without regular employment and economic resources'. However, Austen makes it clear that the encounter is initiated by the hysterical conduct of the young women, and that the gypsies (who consist of half a dozen children and a woman) present very little real threat to the young ladies: 'all clamorous and impertinent in look, though not absolutely in word'. Strikingly, Frank Churchill has been paying yet another visit to Jane Fairfax. His rescue of Harriet incites Emma's final and most painful error.

Miss Smith and Miss Bickerton . . . had walked out together, and taken a road, the Richmond road, which, though apparently public enough for safety, had led them into alarm – About half a mile from Highbury, making a sudden turn . . . they had suddenly perceived at a small distance before them, on a broader patch of greensward by the side, a party of gypsies. [. . .] How the trampers might have behaved, had the young ladies been more courageous, must be doubtful; but such an invitation for attack could not be resisted; and Harriet was soon assailed by half a dozen children, headed by a stout woman and a great boy, all clamorous and impertinent in look, though not absolutely in word. – More and more frightened, she immediately promised them money, and taking out her purse, gave them a shilling, and begged them not to want more, or to use her ill. – She was then able to walk, though but slowly, and was moving away – but her terror and her purse were too tempting, and she was followed, or rather surrounded, by the whole gang, demanding more.

In this state Frank Churchill had found her, she trembling and conditioning, they loud and insolent. By a most fortunate chance his leaving Highbury had been delayed so as to bring him to her assistance at this critical moment. The pleasantness of the morning had induced him to walk forward, and leave his horses to meet him by another road, a mile or two beyond Highbury – and happening to have borrowed a pair of scissars [*sic*] the night before of Miss Bates, and to have forgotten to restore them, he had been obliged to stop at her door, and go in for a few minutes: he was therefore later than he had intended; and being on foot, was unseen by the whole party till almost close to them. The terror which the woman and boy had been creating in Harriet was then their own portion. He had left them completely frightened; and Harriet eagerly clinging to him, and hardly able to speak, had just strength enough to reach Hartfield, before her spirits were quite overcome. It was his idea to bring her to Hartfield: he had thought of no other place. [. . .]

Such an adventure as this, – a fine young man and a lovely young woman thrown together in such a way, could hardly fail of suggesting certain ideas to the coldest heart and the steadiest brain. So Emma thought, at least. Could a linguist, could a grammarian, could even a mathematician have seen what she did, have witnessed their appearance together, and heard their history of it, without feeling that circumstances had been at work to make them peculiarly interesting to each other? – How much more must an imaginist, like herself, be on fire with speculation and foresight! – especially with such a ground-work of anticipation as her mind had already made.

Volume 3, Chapter 4

Emma's final and most painful misunderstanding occurs due to social equivocations which lead her to believe that Harriet is in love with Frank Churchill rather than Mr Knightley. The confusion arises in part because social form dictates that the young women cannot be too explicit, that the man cannot be named. Although Emma encourages Harriet to confess her love, she adds an important codicil: 'Let no name ever pass our lips'. Note the irony contained in her private resolve: 'Plain dealing was always best', and her admonition to Harriet: 'We were very wrong before; we will be cautious now'. The misunderstandings persist as the women, with due propriety, agree upon the superior merits of the 'gentleman' in question for rendering Harriet an elusive 'service'. Emma refers to Frank's rescue of Harriet from the gypsies, whereas Harriet alludes to the far more painful social snub of being 'cut' by Mr Elton at the dance, and saved by Mr Knightley. The irony is intensified by the fact that Emma is determined not to repeat her earlier mistake with Mr Elton, and she is therefore especially self-satisfied with her discretion and 'plain dealing'. Furthermore, Emma's insistence that Harriet is worthy of the match will rebound upon her: 'Harriet, more wonderful things have taken place, there have been matches of greater disparity.'

'Mr Elton indeed!' cried Harriet indignantly. – Oh! No' – and Emma could just catch the words, 'so superior to Mr Elton!' [. . .]

[. . .] – She believed it would be wiser for her to say and know at once, all that she meant to say and know. Plain dealing was always best. She had previously determined how far she would proceed, on any application of the sort; and it would be safer for both, to have the judicious law of her own brain laid down with speed. – She was decided, and thus spoke–

'Harriet, I will not affect to be in doubt of your meaning. Your resolution, or rather your expectation of never marrying, results from an idea that the person whom you might prefer, would be too greatly your superior in situation to think of you. Is not it so?'

'Oh! Miss Woodhouse, believe me I have not the presumption to suppose – Indeed I am not so mad. – But it is a pleasure to me to admire him at a distance – and to think of his infinite superiority to all the rest of the world, with the gratitude, wonder, and veneration, which are so proper, in me especially.'

'I am not at all surprized at you, Harriet. The service he rendered you was enough to warm your heart.'

'Service! oh! it was such an inexpressible obligation! – The very recollection of it, and all that I felt at the time – when I saw him coming – his noble look – and my wretchedness before. Such a change! In one moment such a change! From perfect misery to perfect happiness.'

'It is very natural. It is natural, and it is honourable. – Yes, honourable, I think, to choose so well and so gratefully. – But that it will be a fortunate preference is more than I can promise. I do not advise you to give way to it, Harriet. I do not by any means engage for its being returned. Consider what you are about. Perhaps it will be wisest in you to check your feelings while you can: at any rate do not let them carry you far, unless you are persuaded of his liking you. Be observant of him. Let his behaviour be the guide of your sensations. I give you this caution now, because I shall never speak to you again on the subject. I am determined against all interference. Henceforward I know nothing of the matter. Let no name ever pass our lips. We were very wrong before; we will be cautious now. – He is your superior, no doubt, and there do seem objections and obstacles of a very serious nature; but yet, Harriet, more wonderful things have taken place, there have been matches of greater disparity. But take care of yourself. I would not have you too sanguine; though, however it may end, be assured that your raising your thoughts to *him*, is a mark of good taste which I shall always know how to value.'

Harriet kissed her hand in silent and submissive gratitude. Emma was very decided in thinking such an attachment no bad thing for her friend. It's tendency would be to raise and refine her mind – and it must be saving her from the danger of degradation.

Volume 3, Chapter 5

Earlier in the novel Austen has used charades and riddles to exploit the comic misunderstandings between Emma and Mr Elton. Now she employs word-games to suggest Frank Churchill's duplicity. Mr Knightley's suspicions concerning Frank and Jane are confirmed when he observes the word 'blunder' which Frank shows to Jane. Frank refers to his earlier mistake concerning Mr Perry's carriage, information he has picked up from his correspondence with Jane. When Mr Knightley tells Emma his suspicions, she refuses to believe it. The word-game has a symbolic meaning, for Frank and Jane are playing a 'real' game, and it is left for the others – and the reader – to solve the puzzle. Mr Knightley's perceptiveness is contrasted with Emma's wilful blindness: 'These letters were but the vehicle for gallantry and trick. It was a child's play, chosen to conceal a deeper game on Frank Churchill's part'.

Post-modern critics delight in the novel's verbal dexterity and the slipperi-ness of language that challenges not merely the characters but also the reader. The novel's insistence upon the difficulties of reading is revealed in the text's silence regarding the final word-game. Such critics unravel the inconsistencies and indeterminacies inherent in language and textuality. Valentine Cunningham, for example, plays with the various meanings and interpretations of the word 'Frank', from 'franking' letters, to Frank's lack of frankness (see **p. 84**).

Mr Knightley, who, for some reason best known to himself, had certainly taken an early dislike to Frank Churchill, was only growing to dislike him more. He began to suspect him of some double dealing in his pursuit of Emma. That Emma was his object appeared indisputable. Every thing declared it; his own attentions, his father's hints, his mother-in-law's guarded silence; it was all in unison; words, conduct, discretion, and indiscretion, told the same story. But while so many were devoting him to Emma, and Emma herself making him over to Harriet, Mr Knightley began to suspect him of some inclination to trifle with Jane Fairfax. [. . .]

Frank Churchill placed a word before Miss Fairfax. She gave a slight glance round the table, and applied herself to it. Frank was next to Emma, Jane opposite to them – and Mr Knightley so placed as to see them all; and it was his object to see as much as he could, with as little apparent observation. The word was dis-covered, and with a faint smile pushed away. If meant to be immediately mixed with the others, and buried from sight, she should have looked on the table instead of looking just across, for it was not mixed; and Harriet, eager after every fresh word, and finding out none, directly took it up, and fell to work. She was sitting by Mr Knightley, and turned to him for help. The word was *blunder*; and as Harriet exultingly proclaimed it, there was a blush on Jane's cheek which gave it a meaning not otherwise ostensible. Mr Knightley connected it with the dream; but how it could all be, was beyond his comprehension. How the delicacy, the discretion of his favourite could have been so lain asleep! He feared there must be some decided involvement. Disingenuousness and double-dealing seemed to meet him at every turn. These letters were but the vehicle for gallantry and trick. It was a child's play, chosen to conceal a deeper game on Frank Churchill's part.

With great indignation did he continue to observe him; with great alarm and distrust, to observe also his two blinded companions. He saw a short word prepared for Emma, and given to her with a look sly and demure. He saw that Emma had soon made it out, and found it highly entertaining, though it was something which she judged it proper to appear to censure; for she said, 'Nonsense! for shame!' He heard Frank Churchill next say, with a glance towards Jane, 'I will give it to her – shall I?' – and as clearly heard Emma opposing it with eager laughing warmth. 'No, no, you must not; you shall not, indeed.'

It was done however. This gallant young man, who seemed to love without feeling, and to recommend himself without complaisance, directly handed over the word to Miss Fairfax, and with a particular degree of sedate civility entreated her to study it. Mr Knightley's excessive curiosity to know what this word might be, made him seize every possible moment for darting his eyes towards it, and it was not long before he saw it to be *Dixon*.

Volume 3, Chapter 6

A party is organized to visit Donwell Abbey, the home of Mr Knightley, to pick and eat strawberries.

The stifling heat of the summer's day is emphasized, and Mrs Elton's incessant rattling adds to the sense of claustrophobia. Austen perfectly captures the essence of Mrs Elton's officiousness and her capacity to dominate the scene in her disjointed monologues, expressed in half-sentences, without pause for breath: 'Morning decidedly the best time – never tired – every sort good – hautboy infinitely superior – no comparison – the others hardly eatable – hautboys very scarce –'. Furthermore, Mrs Elton's patronage of Jane Fairfax is seen to be self-aggrandizing and meddlesome: 'Delightful, charming, superior, first circles, spheres, lines, ranks, every thing – and Mrs Elton was wild to have the offer closed with immediately.–.' Mrs Elton's wrong-headed interest in Jane Fairfax highlights Emma's neglect, which Mr Knightley has been quick to notice. However, Mrs Elton's bad rule, as Claudia Johnson has argued, only serves to reflect Emma's rule in a more positive light. Mrs Elton misuses her authority and power to assist in humiliating Harriet and in hastening Jane's assignment as a governess. She expects public acclaim for her acts of social duty, whereas Emma quietly and without fuss performs her social duties. Emma has a 'proper sense of office', as distinguishable from the 'repulsive officiousness' of Mrs Elton (see **p. 80**).

The final passage provides a refreshing contrast, with its patriotic outburst of 'English verdure, English culture, English comfort'. Critics interested in nationalism and patriotism have perceived Mr Knightley and his home as the embodiment of English values. As his name suggests, he is the patron saint and 'knight' of England, St George. Others have suggested that his closeness to the soil, and Donwell Abbey's favourable landscape, suggest harmony with nature.

[. . .] The whole party were assembled, excepting Frank Churchill, who was expected every moment from Richmond; and Mrs Elton, in all her apparatus of happiness, her large bonnet and her basket, was very ready to lead the way in gathering, accepting, or talking – strawberries, and only strawberries, could now be thought or spoken of. – 'The best fruit in England – every body's favourite – always wholesome. – These the finest beds and finest sorts. – Delightful to gather for one's self – the only way of really enjoying them. – Morning decidedly the best time – never tired – every sort good – hautboy[1] infinitely superior – no comparison – the others hardly eatable – hautboys very scarce – Chili preferred – white wood finest flavour of all – price of strawberries in London – abundance about Bristol – Maple Grove – cultivation – beds when to be renewed – gardeners thinking exactly different – no general rule – gardeners never to be put out of their way – delicious fruit – only too rich to be eaten much of – inferior to cherries – currants more refreshing – only objection to gathering strawberries the stooping – glaring sun – tired to death – could bear it no longer – must go and sit in the shade.' [. . .]

Seats tolerably in the shade were found; and now Emma was obliged to over-hear what Mrs Elton and Jane Fairfax were talking of. – A situation, a most desirable situation, was in question. Mrs Elton had received notice of it that morning, and was in raptures. It was not with Mrs Suckling, it was not with Mrs Bragge, but in felicity and splendour it fell short only of them: it was with a cousin of Mrs Bragge, an acquaintance of Mrs Suckling, a lady known at Maple Grove. Delightful, charming, superior, first circles, spheres, lines, ranks, every thing – and Mrs Elton was wild to have the offer closed with immediately. – On her side, all was warmth, energy, and triumph – and she positively refused to take her friend's negative, though Miss Fairfax continued to assure her that she would not at present engage in any thing, repeating the same motives which she had been heard to urge before. [. . .]

It was hot; and after walking some time over the gardens in a scattered, dispersed way, scarcely any three together, they insensibly followed one another to the delicious shade of a broad short avenue of limes, which stretching beyond the garden at an equal distance from the river, seemed the finish of the pleasure grounds. – It led to nothing; nothing but a view at the end over a low stone wall with high pillars, which seemed intended, in their erection, to give the appearance of an approach to the house, which never had been there. Disputable, however, as might be the taste of such a termination, it was in itself a charming walk, and the view which closed it extremely pretty. – The considerable slope, at nearly the foot

1   'Hautboy', the archaic name for the oboe, was also a type of strawberry (as was 'Chili').

of which the Abbey stood, gradually acquired a steeper form beyond its grounds; and at half a mile distant was a bank of considerable abruptness and grandeur, well clothed with wood; – and at the bottom of this bank, favourably placed and sheltered, rose the Abbey-Mill Farm, with meadows in front, and the river making a close and handsome curve around it.

It was a sweet view – sweet to the eye and the mind. English verdure, English culture,[2] English comfort, seen under a sun bright, without being oppressive.

Volume 3, Chapter 7

The party arrange a visit to the local beauty spot, Box Hill (which is still one of Surrey's favourite places for family picnics).

[. . .] Seven miles were travelled in expectation of enjoyment, and every body had a burst of admiration on first arriving; but in the general amount of the day there was deficiency. There was a languor, a want of spirits, a want of union, which could not be got over. They separated too much into parties. The Eltons walked together; Mr Knightley took charge of Miss Bates and Jane; and Emma and Harriet belonged to Frank Churchill. And Mr Weston tried, in vain, to make them harmonize better. It seemed at first an accidental division, but it never materially varied. Mr and Mrs Elton, indeed, showed no unwillingness to mix, and be as agreeable as they could: but during the two whole hours that were spent on the hill, there seemed a principle of separation, between the other parties, too strong for any fine prospects, or any cold collation, or any cheerful Mr Weston, to remove.

At first it was downright dulness [sic] to Emma. She had never seen Frank Churchill so silent and stupid. He said nothing worth hearing – looked without seeing – admired without intelligence – listened without knowing what she said. While he was so dull, it was no wonder that Harriet should be dull likewise, and they were both insufferable.

When they all sat down it was better; to her taste a great deal better, for Frank Churchill grew talkative and gay, making her his first object. Every distinguishing attention that could be paid, was paid to her. To amuse her, and be agreeable in her eyes, seemed all that he cared for – and Emma, glad to be enlivened, not sorry to be flattered, was gay and easy too, and gave him all the friendly encouragement, the admission to be gallant, which she had ever given in the first and most animating period of their acquaintance; but which now, in her own estimation, meant nothing, though in the judgment of most people looking on it must have had such an appearance as no English word but flirtation could very well describe. 'Mr Frank Churchill and Miss Woodhouse flirted together excessively.' They

---

2 'Culture' has the old sense of 'cultivation' (i.e. method of cultivating the soil).

were laying themselves open to that very phrase – and to having it sent off in a letter to Maple Grove by one lady, to Ireland by another. Not that Emma was gay and thoughtless from any real felicity; it was rather because she felt less happy than she had expected. She laughed because she was disappointed; and though she liked him for his attentions, and thought them all, whether in friendship, admiration, or playfulness, extremely judicious, they were not winning back her heart. She still intended him for her friend.

'How much I am obliged to you,' said he, 'for telling me to come to-day! – If it had not been for you, I should certainly have lost all the happiness of this party. I had quite determined to go away again.'

'Yes, you were very cross; and I do not know what about, except that you were too late for the best strawberries. I was a kinder friend than you deserved. But you were humble. You begged hard to be commanded to come.'

'Don't say I was cross. I was fatigued. The heat overcame me.'

'It is hotter to-day.'

'Not to my feelings. I am perfectly comfortable to-day.'

'You are comfortable because you are under command.'

'Your command? – Yes.'

'Perhaps I intended you to say so, but I meant self-command. You had, somehow or other, broken bounds yesterday, and run away from your own management; but to-day you are got back again – and as I cannot be always with you, it is best to believe your temper under your own command rather than mine.'

'It comes to the same thing. I can have no self-command without a motive. You order me, whether you speak or not. And you can be always with me. You are always with me.'

'Dating from three o'clock yesterday. My perpetual influence could not begin earlier, or you would not have been so much out of humour before.'

'Three o'clock yesterday! That is your date. I thought I had seen you first in February.'

'Your gallantry is really unanswerable. But (lowering her voice) – nobody speaks except ourselves, and it is rather too much to be talking nonsense for the entertainment of seven silent people.' [. . .]

'Ladies and gentlemen – I am ordered by Miss Woodhouse to say, that she waves [sic] her right of knowing exactly what you may all be thinking of, and only requires something very entertaining from each of you, in a general way. Here are seven of you, besides myself, (who, she is pleased to say, am very entertaining already,) and she only demands from each of you either one thing very clever, be it prose or verse, original or repeated – or two things moderately clever – or three things very dull indeed, and she engages to laugh heartily at them all.'

'Oh! Very well,' exclaimed Miss Bates, 'then I need not be uneasy. "Three things very dull indeed". That will just do for me, you know. I shall be sure to say three dull things as soon as ever I open my mouth, shan't I? – (looking round with the most good-humoured dependence on every body's assent) – Do not you all think I shall?'

Emma could not resist.

'Ah! ma'am, but there may be a difficulty. Pardon me – but you will be limited as to number – only three at once.'

Miss Bates, deceived by the mock ceremony of her manner, did not immediately catch at her meaning; but, when it burst on her, it could not anger, though a slight blush showed that it could pain her.

'Ah! – well – to be sure. Yes, I see what she means, (turning to Mr Knightley,) and I will try to hold my tongue. I must make myself very disagreeable, or she would not have said such a thing to an old friend.'

A lack of unity and harmony distinguishes the party; Emma and Frank flirt excessively with one another, in part to alleviate the boredom and languor. Emma flirts with Frank, despite believing that Harriet is in love with him. Frank has quarrelled with Jane, and wishes to inflict pain and jealousy on her by his attention to Emma. Emma is inexplicably unhappy, but is receptive to Frank's flattery: 'She laughed because she was disappointed'. Emma's witty but offensive remark to Miss Bates appears to spring from the same ennui and apathy that pervades the group; it is careless and thoughtless, rather than maliciously thought-out: 'Emma could not resist'. The game that Emma proposes is yet another example of the symbolic aspect of games in the novel, and parallels the game that Frank and Jane are secretly playing. There is irony in Emma's wish to know what others are thinking, for Frank and Jane work hard to conceal their true thoughts. Frank and Jane join in a discussion about marriage, which enables them to reproach each other covertly.

'I like your plan,' cried Mr Weston. 'Agreed, agreed. I will do my best. I am making a conundrum. How will a conundrum reckon [. . .] what two letters of the alphabet are there, that express perfection?'

'What two letters! – express perfection! I am sure I do not know'.

'Ah! you will never guess. You, (to Emma), I am certain, will never guess. – I will tell you. – M. and A. – Em – ma. – Do you understand?' [. . .]

Frank's verbal acrobatics reach an unpleasant pitch as he taunts Jane mercilessly, once again using Emma to play off against Jane Fairfax. He uses the discussion about marriage to suggest his regret for the connection he has formed with Jane. Jane responds by suggesting that he is 'weak and irresolute'. With no access to either Jane or Frank's inner thoughts, the reader is left to decode the sub-text of their dialogue. Emma misinterprets Frank's hints regarding a lively wife with hazel eyes to mean Harriet rather than herself, despite the fact that he pointedly states to Emma, 'I shall come to you for my wife'.

The Box Hill scene contains much emotional intensity, and forms the subject of much critical analysis. Julia Prewitt Brown argues that Emma's cruelty to Miss Bates is particularly shocking because she represents a much-loved, comic figure: 'There is something particularly moving and frightening about the rejection of the comic figure in art, such as the rejection of Falstaff or of the clown in a Charlie Chaplin film' (see **p. 69**). However, Mr Knightley's reproach to Emma for humiliating and laughing at Miss Bates makes clear the social inequality of the two women: 'Were she your equal in situation – but, Emma, consider how far this is from being the case. She is poor.' Miss Bates, Jane Fairfax and Harriet Smith are all vulnerable, poor single women in need of protection. Emma temporarily transgresses what Mr Knightley calls the 'something beyond common civility'; perhaps more simply put, kindness. But Emma's is an uncharacteristic act of cruelty, otherwise it would have no effect, and she is swift to see her error: 'How could she have been so brutal, so cruel to Miss Bates!' Furthermore, Emma's essential worthiness, and her capacity to reform are shown in her charitable feelings towards Mr Knightley: 'And how suffer him to leave her without saying one word of gratitude, of concurrence, of common kindness!'

Emma's contrition and her emotional turmoil with regard to Mr Knightley are beautifully expressed in her quiet, uncontrollable tears.

'How many a man has committed himself on a short acquaintance, and rued it all the rest of his life!'

Miss Fairfax, who had seldom spoke before, except among her own confederates, spoke now.

'Such things do occur, undoubtedly.' – She was stopped by a cough. Frank Churchill turned towards her to listen.

'You were speaking,' said he, gravely. She recovered her voice.

'I was only going to observe, that though such unfortunate circumstances do sometimes occur both to men and women, I cannot imagine them to be very frequent. A hasty and imprudent attachment may arise – but there is generally time to recover from it afterwards. I would be understood to mean, that it can be only weak, irresolute characters, (whose happiness must be always at the mercy of chance,) who will suffer an unfortunate acquaintance to be an inconvenience, an oppression for ever.'

He made no answer; merely looked, and bowed in submission; and soon afterwards said, in a lively tone,

'Well, I have so little confidence in my own judgement, that when-ever I marry, I hope somebody will choose my wife for me. Will you? (turning to Emma.) Will you choose a wife for me? – I am sure I should like any body fixed on by you. You provide for the family, you know, (with a smile at his father). Find somebody for me. I am in no hurry. Adopt her, educate her.'

'And make her like myself.'

'By all means, if you can.'

'Very well. I undertake the commission. You shall have a charming wife.'

'She must be very lively, and have hazle [*sic*] eyes. I care for nothing else. I shall go abroad for a couple of years – and when I return, I shall come to you for my wife. Remember.'

Emma was in no danger of forgetting. It was a commission to touch every favourite feeling. Would not Harriet be the very creature described? – Hazle [*sic*] eyes excepted, two years more might make her all that he wished. He might even have Harriet in his thoughts at the moment; who could say? Referring the education to her seemed to imply it. [. . .]

While waiting for the carriage, she found Mr Knightley by her side. He looked around, as if to see that no one were near, and then said,

'Emma, I must once more speak to you as I have been used to do: a privilege rather endured than allowed, perhaps, but I must still use it. I cannot see you acting wrong, without a remonstrance. How could you be so unfeeling to Miss Bates? How could you be so insolent in your wit to a woman of her character, age, and situation? – Emma, I had not thought it possible.'

Emma recollected, blushed, was sorry, but tried to laugh it off.

'Nay, how could I help saying what I did? – Nobody could have helped it. It was not so very bad. I dare say she did not understand me.'

'I assure you she did. She felt your full meaning. She has talked of it since. I wish you could have heard how she talked of it – with what candour and generosity. I wish you could have heard her honouring your forbearance, in being able to pay her such attentions, as she was for ever receiving from yourself and your father, when her society must be so irksome.'

'Oh!' cried Emma, 'I know there is not a better creature in the world: but you must allow, that what is good and what is ridiculous are most unfortunately blended in her.'

'They are blended,' said he, 'I acknowledge; and, were she prosperous, I could allow much for the occasional prevalence of the ridiculous over the good. Were she a woman of fortune, I would leave every harmless absurdity to take its chance, I would not quarrel with you for any liberties of manner. Were she your equal in situation – but, Emma, consider how far this is from being the case. She is poor; she has sunk from the comforts she was born to; and, if she live to old age, must probably sink more. Her situation should secure your compassion. It was badly done, indeed! – You, whom she had known from an infant, whom she had seen grow up from a period when her notice was an honour, to have you now, in thoughtless spirits, and the pride of the moment, laugh at her, humble her – and before her niece, too – and before others, many of whom (certainly *some*,) would be entirely guided by *your* treatment of her. – This is not pleasant to you, Emma – and it is very far from pleasant to me; but I must, I will, – I will tell you truths while I can, satisfied with proving myself your friend by very faithful counsel, and trusting that you will some time or other do me greater justice than you can do now.'

While they talked, they were advancing towards the carriage; it was ready; and, before she could speak again, he had handed her in. He had misinterpreted the feelings which had kept her face averted, and her tongue motionless. They were combined only of anger against herself, mortification, and deep concern. She had not been able to speak; and, on entering the carriage, sunk back for a moment overcome – then reproaching herself for having taken no leave, making no acknowledgement, parting in apparent sullenness, she looked out with voice and hand eager to show a difference; but it was just too late. He had turned away, and the horses were in motion. She continued to look back, but in vain; and soon, with what appeared unusual speed, they were half way down the hill, and every thing left far behind. She was vexed beyond what could have been expressed – almost beyond what she could conceal. Never had she felt so agitated, mortified, grieved, at any circumstance in her life. She was most forcibly struck. The truth of his representation there was no denying. She felt it at her heart. How could she have been so brutal, so cruel to Miss Bates! – How could she have exposed herself to such ill opinion in any one she valued! And how suffer him to leave her without saying one word of gratitude, of concurrence, of common kindness!

Time did not compose her. As she reflected more, she seemed but to feel it more. She never had been so depressed. Happily it was not necessary to speak. There was only Harriet, who seemed not in spirits herself, fagged, and very willing to be silent; and Emma felt the tears running down her cheeks almost all the way home, without being at any trouble to check them, extraordinary as they were.

Volume 3, Chapter 11

After the news of Frank and Jane's engagement breaks, Emma once again finds herself in the position of having to disappoint Harriet's hopes. To Emma's horror, she discovers that the object of Harriet's affection is not Frank Churchill, but Mr Knightley. When the mistake comes to light, it is the catalyst for Emma's double epiphany, the revelation of her own love for Knightley and the realization of her own wrong-doing.

Emma's repentance is all-encompassing. She realizes that she has been 'universally mistaken': 'With insufferable vanity had she believed herself in the secret of everybody's feelings; with unpardonable arrogance proposed to arrange everybody's destiny. She was proved to have been universally mistaken; and she had not quite done nothing – for she had done mischief. She had brought evil on Harriet, on herself, and she too much feared, on Mr Knightley.'

The theme of intermarriage between the social classes comes full circle (the novel begins with the marriage of the rich tradesman, Mr Weston, to a governess) when Emma is faced with what she thinks is the probability, not merely the possibility between illegitimate Harriet and the well-born Mr Knightley: 'Could it be? – No; it was impossible. And yet it was far, very far, from impossible'. Emma's capacity for self-knowledge is revealed in her admission that she has been responsible for giving Harriet notions of great expectations: 'Who but herself had taught her, that she was to elevate herself if possible, and that her claims were great to a high worldly establishment?'

'Have you any idea of Mr Knightley's returning your affection?'

'Yes,' replied Harriet modestly, but not fearfully – 'I must say that I have.'

Emma's eyes were instantly withdrawn; and she sat silently meditating, in a fixed attitude, for a few minutes. A few minutes were sufficient for making her acquainted with her own heart. A mind like hers, once opening to suspicion, made rapid progress. She touched – she admitted – she acknowledged the whole truth. Why was it so much worse that Harriet should be in love with Mr Knightley, than with Frank Churchill? Why was the evil so dreadfully increased by Harriet's having some hope of a return? It darted through her, with the speed of an arrow, that Mr Knightley must marry no one but herself!

Her own conduct, as well as her own heart, was before her in the same few minutes. She saw it all with a clearness which had never blessed her before. How improperly had she been acting by Harriet! How inconsiderate, how indelicate, how irrational, how unfeeling had been her conduct! What blindness, what madness, had led her on! It struck her with dreadful force, and she was ready to give it every bad name in the world. Some portion of respect for herself, however, in spite of all these demerits – some concern for her own appearance, and a strong sense of justice by Harriet – (there would be no need of *compassion* to the girl who believed herself loved by Mr Knightley – but justice required that she should not be made unhappy by any coldness now,) gave Emma the resolution to sit and endure farther with calmness, with even apparent kindness. – For her own advantage indeed, it was fit that the utmost extent of Harriet's hopes should be enquired into; and Harriet had done nothing to forfeit the regard and interest which had been so voluntarily formed and maintained – or to deserve to be slighted by the person, whose counsels had never led her right. – Rousing from reflection, therefore, and subduing her emotion, she turned to Harriet again, and, in a more inviting accent, renewed the conversation; for as to the subject which had first introduced it, the wonderful story of Jane Fairfax, that was quite sunk and lost. – Neither of them thought but of Mr Knightley and themselves.

Harriet, who had been standing in no unhappy reverie, was yet very glad to be called from it, by the now encouraging manner of such a judge, and such a friend as Miss Woodhouse, and only wanted invitation, to give the history of her hopes with great, though trembling delight. – Emma's tremblings as she asked, and as she listened, were better concealed than Harriet's, but they were not less. Her voice was not unsteady; but her mind was in all the perturbation that such a development of self, such a burst of threatening evil, such a confusion of sudden and perplexing emotions, must create. – She listened with much inward suffering, but with great outward patience, to Harriet's detail. [. . .]

The rest of the day, the following night, were hardly enough for her thoughts. – She was bewildered amidst the confusion of all that had rushed on her within the last few hours. Every moment had brought a fresh surprise; and every surprise must be a matter of humiliation to her. – How to understand it all! How to understand the deceptions she had been thus practising on herself, and living under! – the blunders, the blindness of her own head and heart! – she sat still, she walked about, she tried her own room, she tried the shrubbery – in every place, every posture, she perceived that she had acted most weakly; that she had been imposed on by others in a most mortifying degree; that she had been imposing on herself in a degree yet more mortifying; that she was wretched, and should probably find this day but the beginning of wretchedness.

To understand, thoroughly understand her own heart, was the first endeavour. To that point went every leisure moment which her father's claims on her allowed, and every moment of involuntary absence of mind.

How long had Mr Knightley been so dear to her, as every feeling declared him now to be? When had his influence, such influence begun? – When had he succeeded to that place in her affection, which Frank Churchill had once, for a short period, occupied? – She looked back; she compared the two – compared them, as they had always stood in her estimation, from the time of the latter's becoming known to her – and as they must at any time have been compared by her, had it – oh! had it, by any blessed felicity, occurred to her, to institute the comparison. – She saw that there never had been a time when she did not consider Mr Knightley as infinitely the superior, or when his regard for her had not been infinitely the most dear. She saw, that in persuading herself, in fancying, in acting to the contrary, she had been entirely under a delusion, totally ignorant of her own heart – and, in short, that she had never really cared for Frank Churchill at all!

This was the conclusion of the first series of reflection. This was the knowledge of herself, on the first question of inquiry, which she reached; and without being long in reaching it. – She was most sorrowfully indignant; ashamed of every sensation but the one revealed to her – her affection for Mr Knightley. – Every other part of her mind was disgusting.

With insufferable vanity had she believed herself in the secret of everybody's feelings; with unpardonable arrogance proposed to arrange everybody's destiny. She was proved to have been universally mistaken; and she had not quite done nothing – for she had done mischief. She had brought evil on Harriet, on herself, and she too much feared, on Mr Knightley. – Were this most unequal of all connexions to take place, on her must rest all the reproach of having given it a beginning; for his attachment, she must believe to be produced only by a con-sciousness of Harriet's; – and even were this not the case, he would never have known Harriet at all but for her folly.

Mr Knightley and Harriet Smith! – It was an union to distance every wonder of the kind. – The attachment of Frank Churchill and Jane Fairfax became com-monplace, threadbare, stale in the comparison, exciting no surprise, presenting no disparity, affording nothing to be said or thought. – Mr Knightley and Harriet Smith! – Such an elevation on her side! Such a debasement on his! – It was horrible to Emma to think how it must sink him in the general opinion, to foresee the smiles, the sneers, the merriment it would prompt at his expense; the mortifi-cation and disdain of his brother, the thousand inconveniences to himself. – Could it be? – No; it was impossible. And yet it was far, very far, from impossible. – Was it a new circumstance for a man of first-rate abilities to be captivated by very inferior powers? Was it new for one, perhaps too busy to seek, to be the prize of a girl who would seek him? – Was it new for any thing in this world to be unequal, inconsistent, incongruous – or for chance and circumstance (as second causes) to direct the human fate?

Oh! had she never brought Harriet forward! Had she left her where she ought, and where he had told her she ought! – Had she not, with a folly which no tongue could express, prevented her marrying the unexceptionable young man who would have made her happy and respectable in the line of life to which she ought to belong – all would have been safe; none of this dreadful sequel would have been.

How Harriet could ever have had the presumption to raise her thoughts to Mr Knightley! – How she could dare to fancy herself the chosen of such a man till actually assured of it! – But Harriet was less humble, had fewer scruples than formerly. – Her inferiority, whether of mind or situation, seemed little felt. – She had seemed more sensible of Mr Elton's being to stoop in marrying her, than she now seemed of Mr Knightley's. – Alas! was not that her own doing too? Who had been at pains to give Harriet notions of self-consequence but herself? – Who but herself had taught her, that she was to elevate herself if possible, and that her claims were great to a high worldly establishment? – If Harriet, from being humble, were grown vain, it was her doing too.

Volume 3, Chapter 13

Emma's final misunderstanding is cleared up when she discovers that Mr Knightley is not in love with Harriet, as she fears, but with Emma herself.

Mr Knightley declares to Emma on Box Hill, 'I will tell you truths while I can.' There is only one final agonizing encounter when they fail to communicate fully, a last misunderstanding when each believes the other to be in love with someone else. But this is short-lived, for Emma, having begged Mr Knightley not to speak of his love (little realizing that it is herself), selflessly puts his feeling first: 'cost it what it would, she would listen'. When the misunderstanding is finally resolved, he shows his characteristic awkwardness with the language of sentiment: 'I cannot make speeches . . . if I loved you less, I might be able to talk about it more.' Similarly, Austen does not let her lovers indulge in sentimental talk: 'What did she say? – Just what she ought, of course. A lady always does. –.' Here, the authorial voice reasserts itself on the narrative, and Emma's internal thoughts are rendered in an extraordinary interior monologue, as unspoken thoughts and feelings flash through her mind: 'While he spoke, Emma's mind was most busy, and, with all the wonderful velocity of thought, had been able – and yet without losing a word – to catch and comprehend the exact truth of the whole; to see that Harriet's hopes had been entirely groundless, a mistake, a delusion, as complete a delusion as any of her own – that Harriet was nothing; that she was every thing herself'.

This insight into Emma's mind is an innovation that seems closer to the 'stream of consciousness' of modern writers such as Virginia Woolf than to eighteenth-century writers. Emma is far too honest to admit to herself that she feels real despair for Harriet's loss of Mr Knightley: 'She felt for Harriet, with pain and with contrition; but no flight of generosity run mad, opposing all that could be probable or reasonable, entered her brain.' Finally, Mr Knightley makes the ultimate sacrifice in moving into Emma's home, despite his earlier insistence that 'A man would always wish to give a woman a better home than he takes from her'. For feminist scholar Claudia Johnson, Mr Knightley's sacrifice is the ultimate example of his sanction of Emma's rule: 'The conclusion which seemed tamely and placidly conservative thus takes an unexpected turn, as the guarantor of order himself cedes a considerable portion of the power which custom has allowed him to expect. In moving to Hartfield, Knightley is sharing *her* home, and in placing himself within her domain, Knightley gives his blessing to her rule' (see p. 81).

They walked together. He was silent. She thought he was often looking at her, and trying for a fuller view of her face than it suited her to give. And this belief produced another dread. Perhaps he wanted to speak to her, of his attachment to Harriet; he might be watching for encouragement to begin. [. . .]

'But if you have any wish to speak openly to me as a friend, or to ask my opinion of any thing that you may have in contemplation – as a friend, indeed, you may command me. – I will hear whatever you like. I will tell you exactly what I think.'

'As a friend!' repeated Mr Knightley. – 'Emma, that I fear is a word – No, I have no wish – Stay, yes, why should I hesitate? – I have gone too far already for concealment. – Emma, I accept your offer – Extraordinary as it may seem, I accept it, and refer myself to you as a friend. – Tell me, then, have I no chance of ever succeeding?'

He stopped in his earnestness to look the question, and the expression of his eyes overpowered her.

'My dearest Emma,' said he, 'for dearest you will always be, whatever the event of this hour's conversation, my dearest, most beloved Emma – tell me at once. Say "No," if it is to be said.' – She could really say nothing. – 'You are silent,' he cried, with great animation; 'absolutely silent! at present I ask no more.'

Emma was almost ready to sink under the agitation of this moment. The dread of being awakened from the happiest dream, was perhaps the most prominent feeling.

'I cannot make speeches, Emma:' – he soon resumed; and in a tone of such sincere, decided, intelligible tenderness as was tolerably convincing. – 'If I loved you less, I might be able to talk about it more. But you know what I am. – You hear nothing but truth from me. – I have blamed you, and lectured you, and you have borne it as no other woman in England would have borne it. – Bear with the truths I would tell you now, dearest Emma, as well as you have borne with them.

The manner, perhaps, may have as little to recommend them. God knows, I have been a very indifferent lover. – But you understand me. – Yes, you see, you understand my feelings – and will return them if you can. At present, I ask only to hear, once to hear your voice.'

While he spoke, Emma's mind was most busy, and, with all the wonderful velocity of thought, had been able – and yet without losing a word – to catch and comprehend the exact truth of the whole; to see that Harriet's hopes had been entirely groundless, a mistake, a delusion, as complete a delusion as any of her own – that Harriet was nothing; that she was every thing herself; that what she had been saying relative to Harriet had been all taken as the language of her own feelings; and that her agitation, her doubts, her reluctance, her discouragement, had been all received as discouragement from herself. – And not only was there time for these convictions, with all their glow of attendant happiness; there was time also to rejoice that Harriet's secret had not escaped her, and to resolve that it need not and should not. – It was all the service she could now render her poor friend; for as to any of that heroism of sentiment which might have prompted her to entreat him to transfer his affection from herself to Harriet, as infinitely the most worthy of the two – or even the more simple sublimity of resolving to refuse him at once and for ever, without vouchsafing any motive, because he could not marry them both, Emma had it not. She felt for Harriet, with pain and with contrition; but no flight of generosity run mad, opposing all that could be probable or reasonable, entered her brain. She had led her friend astray, and it would be a reproach to her for ever; but her judgment was as strong as her feelings, and as strong as it had ever been before, in reprobating any such alliance for him, as most unequal and degrading. Her way was clear, though not quite smooth. – She spoke then, on being so entreated. – What did she say? – Just what she ought, of course. A lady always does. – She said enough to show there need not be despair – and to invite him to say more himself. He *had* despaired at one period; he had received such an injunction to caution and silence, as for the time crushed every hope; – she had begun by refusing to hear him. – The change had perhaps been somewhat sudden; – her proposal of taking another turn, her renewing the conversation which she had just put an end to, might be a little extraordinary! – She felt its inconsistency; but Mr Knightley was so obliging as to put up with it, and seek no farther explanation.

Seldom, very seldom, does complete truth belong to any human disclosure; seldom can it happen that something is not a little disguised, or a little mistaken; but where, as in this case, though the conduct is mistaken, the feelings are not, it may not be very material.

Volume 3, Chapter 18

The novel comes full circle with the union of Harriet Smith and Robert Martin. Emma accepts that she has been wrong to look down on Martin and Mr Knightley accepts that he under-rated Harriet Smith. There is great humour and understanding in Emma's representation of Harriet's fickle emotions: 'Such a heart – such a Harriet!' Emma and Mr Knightley look forward to a relationship distinguished by openness and honesty. It may be worth considering however, that Emma continues to conceal secrets from Mr Knightley. She has never disclosed her suspicions about Jane and Mr Dixon, and she has not disclosed Harriet's secret that she loved Mr Knightley. Whether or not Emma finally does reveal the whole truth to Mr Knightley is left open. But perhaps the ambiguity should come as no surprise, for the authorial voice has warned the reader of the impossibility of 'complete truth': 'Seldom, very seldom, does complete truth belong to any human disclosure; seldom can it happen that something is not a little disguised, or a little mistaken; but where, as in this case, though the conduct is mistaken, the feelings are not, it may not be very material.'

'I am perfectly satisfied,' replied Emma, with the brightest smiles, 'and most sincerely wish them happy.'

'You are materially changed since we talked on this subject before.'

'I hope so – for at that time I was a fool.'

'And I am changed also; for I am now very willing to grant you all Harriet's good qualities. I have taken some pains for your sake, and for Robert Martin's sake, (whom I have always had reason to believe as much in love with her as ever,) to get acquainted with her. I have often talked to her a good deal. You must have seen that I did. Sometimes, indeed, I have thought you were half suspecting me of pleading poor Martin's cause, which was never the case: but, from all my observations, I am convinced of her being an artless, amiable girl, with very good notions, very seriously good principles, and placing her happiness in the affections and utility of domestic life. – Much of this, I have no doubt, she may thank you for.'

'Me!' cried Emma, shaking her head. – 'Ah! poor Harriet!'

She checked herself, however, and submitted quietly to a little more praise than she deserved.

Their conversation was soon afterwards closed by the entrance of her father. She was not sorry. She wanted to be alone. Her mind was in a state of flutter and wonder, which made it impossible for her to be collected. She was in dancing, singing, exclaiming spirits; and till she had moved about, and talked to herself, and laughed and reflected, she could be fit for nothing rational.

Her father's business was to announce James's being gone out to put the horses to, preparatory to their now daily drive to Randall's; and she had, therefore, an immediate excuse for disappearing.

The joy, the gratitude, the exquisite delight of her sensations may be imagined. The sole grievance and alloy thus removed in the prospect of Harriet's welfare, she was really in danger of becoming too happy for security. – What had she to wish for? Nothing, but to grow more worthy of him, whose intentions and judgment had been ever so superior to her own. Nothing, but that the lessons of her past folly might teach her humility and circumspection in future.

Serious she was, very serious in her thankfulness, and in her resolutions; and yet there was no preventing a laugh, sometimes in the very midst of them. She must laugh at such a close! Such an end of the doleful disappointment of five weeks back! Such a heart – such a Harriet!

Now there would be pleasure in her returning. – Every thing would be a pleasure. It would be a great pleasure to know Robert Martin.

High in the rank of her most serious and heartfelt felicities, was the reflection that all necessity of concealment from Mr Knightley would soon be over. The disguise, equivocation, mystery, so hateful to her to practise, might soon be over. She could now look forward to giving him that full and perfect confidence which her disposition was most ready to welcome as a duty.

4

Further Reading

Further Reading

Recommended Editions

The standard scholarly edition is *Emma: Oxford Illustrated Jane Austen*, ed. R. W. Chapman (Oxford: Oxford University Press, 1988), which was originally published in 1933. This lists all the typographical errors in the first edition. But since no manuscript survives and there was no second edition in Austen's lifetime, there is no major textual problem. All the modern paperback student editions follow either Chapman or the first edition itself. The following are particularly recommended for their introductions and notes:

Emma, ed. James Kinsley, with introduction by Terry Castle (Oxford World's Classics, 1998).
Emma, ed. Fiona Stafford, with introduction by Tony Tanner (Penguin Classics, 2003).
Emma, with introduction by Marilyn Butler (Everyman's Library Classics, 1991).

More expensive, but with useful additional critical materials:

Emma, ed. Stephen M. Parrish (Norton Critical Edition, 1993).
Emma, ed. Alistair M. Duckworth (Bedford/St Martin's Press, 2001).

Further Reading

The best way of deepening one's understanding of Jane Austen is to read her other novels. Special insight into her comic art is provided by her 'juvenilia', usefully collected in:

Jane Austen, *Catharine and Other Writings*, ed. Margaret Anne Doody and Douglas Murray (Oxford World's Classics, 1993).

The next step should be to read some of the novels of her female contemporaries, perhaps beginning with the notably innovative and influential tale of 'a young woman's entrance into the world':

Fanny Burney, *Evelina*, ed. Margaret Anne Doody (1778; Penguin Classics, 1994).

Next, a novel of class and courtship much admired by Austen:

Maria Edgeworth, *Belinda*, ed. Kathryn Kirkpatrick (1801; Oxford World's Classics, 1994).

Austen's own voice is heard to great effect in her

Letters, ed. Deirdre le Faye (3rd edn, Oxford University Press, 1995).

The most readable modern biography of her is:

Claire Tomalin, *Jane Austen: A Life* (Viking, 1997).

A fuller account of her literary context is provided by:

Jan Fergus, *Jane Austen: A Literary Life* (Macmillan, 1991).

Other books which might have been represented in this sourcebook if more space had been available include:

John Burrows, *Computation into Criticism: Jane Austen's Language* (Oxford University Press, 1986) [a fascinating study of the distinctive language habits of each major character in the novels].

Margaret Kirkham, *Jane Austen: Feminism and Fiction* (Athlone Press, 1997) [a good example of undogmatic feminist criticism].

Mary Lascelles, *Jane Austen and Her Art* (Clarendon Press, 1939) [the earliest full-length account of Austen as a conscious artist, and still worth reading].

Roger Sales, *Jane Austen and Representations of Regency England* (Routledge, 1996) [a lively example of 'New Historicist' criticism that illuminates the novels in the context of the social and cultural history of their time].

A sense of changing fashions in Austen criticism may be gained from a comparison of the following two books:

David Lodge (ed.), *Jane Austen: 'Emma'. A Casebook* (Macmillan, 1968).

David Monaghan (ed.), *Jane Austen: 'Emma'. A New Casebook* (Macmillan, 1992).

The history of the 'Janeite' phenomenon is fascinatingly analysed in:

Claudia L. Johnson, 'The Divine Miss Jane: Jane Austen, Janeites, and the

Discipline of Novel Studies', *Boundary 2: An International Journal of Literature and Culture*, vol. 23 (1996), pp. 143–63, reprinted in *Janeites: Austen's Disciples and Devotees*, ed. Deirdre Lynch (Princeton University Press, 2000), pp. 25–44.

The translation of Austen from page to screen, and in particular the spate of 1990s Hollywood versions, is surveyed and interestingly analysed in:

Linda Troost and Sayre Greenfield (eds), *Jane Austen in Hollywood* (University Press of Kentucky, 1998).

There is a wealth of useful information, both scholarly and critical, in:

David Grey (ed.), *The Jane Austen Handbook* (Athlone Press, 1986).

An interesting collection of essays on the Box Hill episode is available online at www.rc.umd.edu/praxis/boxhill/. For other internet resources, begin at www.pemberley.com – a charming mixture of the academic and the 'Janeite' – which has hypertext links to many other Austen sites.

Index

sales figures 2
'Sanditon' 10, 16, 32
satire 53, 54, 128
Schorer, Mark 61–2, 84
science 7
Scott, Sir Walter 2, 10–11, 16, 32, 33, 37, 38–40, 42, 43, 92–3
Scrutiny 53
Sense and Sensibility 2n, 7, 9, 14, 15, 38, 96
sensibility 7, 8, 10, 20, 84, 85–6, 92
sentimental novels 7, 19–20, 22, 38, 40, 116; *see also* romantic novels
Shakespeare, William 2, 6, 31, 43, 44, 46, 47, 52, 55, 69, 140
Shelley, Mary 13, 14, 16
Shelley, Percy Bysshe 15
Sheridan, Richard Brinsley 6, 7, 12
shopping *see* consumerism
Silverstone, Alicia 94
Simpson, Richard 33, 45–7, 48
single women *see* unmarried women
slave trade 9, 14, 15, 88, 128, 129n; *see also* women, as slaves
Smith, Adam 12
snobbery 2, 35, 57, 58, 59, 60, 87, 120, 123
social mobility 8, 35, 69, 86, 89
social order 73–4, 81, 128, 142; *see also* class
social problems 46, 47
social values 65, 66, 69
solipsism 78, 79
Southam, Brian C. 10n, 17, 19, 33n, 38, 90–2
Southampton 12, 15
Spenser, Edmund 93n
spinsters *see* unmarried women
Stafford, Fiona 153
Stern, Miss 55
Steventon 5, 6, 12, 13
'stream of consciousness' 146
structuralism 35
subscription libraries 5, 6
subversiveness 31, 34, 36, 53, 57
Susan 14, 15
Sutherland, Kathryn 99n
Symington, J. A. 42n

Tanner, Tony 153

television 93–4, 155
theatre *see* plays
Thompson, James 78–9
Todd, Janet 24
Tomalin, Claire 154
Toryism 31, 35, 36, 66n, 75
trade 86, 87, 123, 128
traditional values 31, 34, 35, 65, 66
Trafalgar, battle of (1805) 15
Trilling, Lionel 34, 59–60
Troost, Linda 94, 95, 155
trophies 76

unmarried women 9, 21, 23, 67, 68, 104, 115, 128, 140

vulnerability *see* women, vulnerability; unmarried women

Walpole, Horace 93
Walpole, Robert 93n
Waterloo, battle of (1815) 8, 16, 56
'Watsons, The' 9, 15, 21–2
Watt, Ian 34, 54, 61
Watt, James 12
Wellington, Arthur Wellesley, Duke of 16
West, Jane 66
Williams, Raymond 35
Williams, W. S. 42
Wilson, Edmund 34, 54–5, 57, 84, 85
Wiltshire, John 81–3
Winchester 16
Wise, T. J. 42n
wit 8, 23, 27, 31, 102
Wollstonecraft, Mary 9, 13, 14, 24–5, 36, 66
women 101n; domestic 36, 77; education 27; friendships 27; and power 36, 58, 67, 80–1; rights and duties 24–5; as slaves 9, 24–5, 75, 88, 128; speech modes 77–8; unmarried *see* unmarried women; vulnerability 70–1; *see also* lesbianism; marriage
Woolf, Virginia 5, 7, 146
word-games 31, 35–6, 65, 70, 83, 113, 117, 125, 134
Wordsworth, William 10, 11, 14, 16, 32–3, 35n